Cake Pops, Cupcakes

& Other Petite Sweets

Cake Pops, Cupcakes

& Other Petite Sweets

Sweet and Simple Recipes to Turn Your Kitchen Into a Home Bake Shop

Edited by Peg Couch

FOX CHAPEL
PUBLISHING

© 2012 by Fox Chapel Publishing Company, Inc., 1970 Broad Street, East Petersburg, PA 17520

Recipe selection, design, and book design © Fox Chapel Publishing.
Recipes and photography © G&R Publishing DBA CQ Products.

ISBN 978-1-56523-739-1

Library of Congress Cataloging-in-Publication Data

Cake pops, cupcakes, and other petite sweets.
      p. cm.
   Includes index.
   ISBN 978-1-56523-739-1
   1. Baking. I. Fox Chapel Publishing.
   TX763.C195 2012
   641.81'5--dc23
                        2012007872

To learn more about the other great books from Fox Chapel Publishing, or to find a retailer near you, call toll-free 800-457-9112 or visit us at www.FoxChapelPublishing.com.

Note to Authors: We are always looking for talented authors to write new books. Please send a brief letter describing your idea to Acquisition Editor, 1970 Broad Street, East Petersburg, PA 17520.

Printed in China
First printing

Introduction

If you have a persistent sweet tooth or are looking for a fresh, new recipe to wow guests at your next party, the parade of delicious desserts starts here! With unique flavor combinations and helpful serving hints, these desserts were meant to impress—and they will. For all you party planners out there, make an impressive dessert tray full of cake pops and other tiny bites that will have your guests clamoring for more. Delectable dessert morsels like Tiki Bar Volcanoes (page 42), Rainbow Blondie Party Pops (page 37), and Chocolate-Covered Cheesecake Pops (page 10), found in the first section, will make you the talk of the town. If you're looking for the comfort of classic dessert flavors, whip up some traditional cupcakes, cookies, and muffins like those found in the second, third, and fourth sections of the book. Indulge in Brownie Peanut Butter Cupcakes (page 63), Easy Pinwheel Cookies (page 73), and Blueberry Streusel Muffins (page 91). Want to explore some fanciful flavors? Try Meringue-Topped Raspberry Cupcakes (page 66), Big Dip Biscotti (page 70), or Pistachio Muffins (page 99). And don't forget to check out the fifth section, which is full of pies, parfaits, and ice cream recipes perfect for a summertime get-together. Prepare for your kitchen to undergo a transformation from ordinary dessert factory to home bake shop, because once you make one of these fabulous recipes, you'll never want to stop. So fire up the oven and let the baking begin!

Table of Contents

Cake Pops & Bites. 8

Tingly Mint Fudge 9
Chocolate-Covered Cheesecake Pops . . 10
Peppermint Brownie Pops 12
Milk Chocolate Malt Cheesecakes. 14
Surprise Brownie Babies. 15
Orange-Kissed Brownie Wedges 16
Cranberry Blondies 17
Chocolate & Mint Cheesecake Bites . . . 18
Bon Bon Delights 19
Peanut Butter Cheesecake Pops 20
Raspberry Swirl Cheesecake Cubes . . . 22
Double-Dipped Blondie Pops 24
Dainty Mocha Cheesecake Baskets. . . . 26
No-Bake Mandarin Orange Tartlets . . . 27
Tantalizing Truffles 28
Fudge Jewels. 29
Triple Chocolate Cheesecake Wedges . 30
Brownie Bomb Pops. 32
Chocolate-Covered Cherry
Cheesecake Bits. 34
No-Bake Pumpkin Wedges. 35
Strawberry Cheesecake Minis 36
Rainbow Blondie Party Pops. 37
Cookie Crust Cheesecakes 38
Lime Cheesecake Mini Tarts 40
Tiki Bar Volcanoes 42
Black & White Cut-Ups 44

Triangle Treats 45
Tiny Turtle Cheesecakes. 46
Blueberry Cheesecake Fudge Minis . . . 47
German Chocolate Brownie Pops 48
Little Rocky Roads 50

Cupcakes. 51

Milky Way Sweetcakes 52
Carnival Poke Cupcakes 53
Luscious Lemonade Cupcakes. 54
Scrumptious Strawberry Cupcakes. . . . 55
Mandarin Coconut Delights. 56
Orange Kiss-Me Cupcakes 57
Nutty Banana-Maple Cupcakes. 58
Sweetheart Chocolate Cupcakes. 59
Traditional Red Velvet Cupcakes. 60
Out of the Blue Coconut Snowballs . . . 61
Cookies & Cream Cupcakes 62
Brownie Peanut Butter Cupcakes 63
Chocolate Cherry Cupcakes. 64
Cappuccino Cupcakes. 65
Meringue-Topped
Raspberry Cupcakes 66
Cookie Dough Cupcakes. 67

Cookies, Cakes, Cheesecakes & Bars 68

Cocoa Cream Thumbprints 69
Big Dip Biscotti. 70
Iced Treasures 71
Sweet Cookie Pizza 72
Easy Pinwheel Cookies 73
Chocolate Cream Mallows 74
Sweet Pumpkin Roll 75
Love-Filled Cake Roll. 76
Cookies & Cream Cake 77
Slow Cooker Puddin' Cake 78
Irish Cream Cheesecake. 79
"Oh My!" Cheesecake Pie 80
Lemon Luscious Cheesecake. 81
Frosty Blueberry Cream 82
Frosted Shortbread Squares. 83
Chippy Bars 84
Dreamy Yum Yums 85

Muffins 86

Double Chocolate Chunk Muffins 87
Sour Cherry Muffins 88
Pumpkin Muffins with Vanilla Icing . . . 89
Rhubarb Buttermilk Muffins 90
Blueberry Streusel Muffins. 91
Java Mocha Muffins. 92
Oatmeal Raisin Cookie Muffins 93
Chunky Apple Breakfast Muffins 94
Toffee Crunch Muffins 95

Raspberry Lime Muffins 96
Cheesy Sun-Dried Tomato Muffins 97
Glazed Lemon Poppy Seed Muffins. . . . 98
Pistachio Muffins. 99
Dark Chocolate
Banana Nut Muffins 100
Hawaiian Island Muffins 101

Pies, Parfaits & Ice Cream 102

Heart's Delight Pie. 103
Cloud Nine Pie 104
Key Lime Pie. 105
Dreamy Creamy Tart. 106
Creamy Mousse Pie. 107
White Chocolate Decadence 108
Double Rich Mousse 109
Banana Pudding Parfaits 110
Chippy Cream Sandwiches 111
Luscious Layered Bombe 112
Ice Cream Sandwiches 113
Lovely Freezer Pleaser. 114
Cool Cookie Pops 115
Berry Creamwiches. 116
Peanut Butter Cup Milkshake 117

Garnishing with Flair! . . 118

Index. 119

Cake Pops & Bites

Bite-size morsels are the answer to dessert deprivation! Guests can indulge in more than one tiny treat without guilt. And preparation is easy because these small desserts generally bake more quickly than the full-size versions. Keep the following in mind when trying the pops recipes: White *lollipop* sticks are generally about 4" long and are heat-safe; plastic ones should be inserted after baking. White *cookie* sticks are somewhat thicker. These and other supplies can be found wherever baking and cake decorating supplies are sold. Always purchase items that are food-safe.

For tips on creating cheesecakes, refer to page 68. Below are helpful hints for making terrific brownies.

Brownie Tips

✳ In place of specialty baking pans, brownies may be baked in round, square or rectangular pans and then cut with a knife or cookie cutters into desired shapes before decorating. Lining pans with aluminum foil or parchment paper before baking allows easy removal from the pan for trouble-free cutting.

✳ Use a plastic knife to cut dense, chewy brownies.

✳ Miniature cookie cutters can be used to cut brownies, and cheesecakes, into fun shapes. Metal petit four cutters are approximately 1¼" in diameter and 2" tall, making them perfect for tiny desserts.

✳ Brownies are done when a toothpick inserted halfway between the center and edge of pan comes out with few or no crumbs.

✳ If brownies do not immediately adhere to lollipop sticks when making pops, simply press the brownie gently against the stick or refrigerate pops for 30 minutes until adhered.

✳ For easier handling, refrigerate brownie cutouts on the sticks before dipping, drizzling or coating with melted mixtures.

✳ Place waxed paper under a cooling rack to catch the drips when drizzling brownies with icing or melted almond bark. If coated brownies are set directly on waxed paper to dry, coating may puddle. Carefully cut away the excess coating after it dries.

Tingly Mint Fudge

Makes 36 pieces

Ingredients

1 (7 oz.) jar marshmallow creme

1½ C. sugar

⅔ C. evaporated milk

¼ C. butter

1 (12 oz.) pkg. semi-sweet chocolate chips

1 tsp. vanilla extract

1 C. chopped Fudge Shoppe Grasshopper cookies

Preparation

Line an 8" x 8" square pan with aluminum foil, extending foil over ends of pan. Lightly coat with nonstick cooking spray; set aside. In a medium saucepan over medium heat, combine marshmallow creme, sugar, evaporated milk and butter. Cook, stirring constantly, until mixture comes to a full boil. Reduce heat to medium-low. Gently boil for 4 minutes, stirring constantly. Remove from heat. Stir in chocolate chips and vanilla until chips are melted. Fold in chopped cookies. Spread in prepared pan; cool. Refrigerate until firm before cutting into squares.

Chocolate-Covered Cheesecake Pops

Makes about 2½ dozen

Filling

2 (8 oz.) pkgs. cream cheese, softened

¾ C. sugar

1½ T. flour

2 eggs

1 egg yolk

½ C. sour cream

1½ tsp. vanilla extract

1½ tsp. lemon juice

Coating & Garnishes

⅓ C. white candy melts wafers (or almond bark)

1 (12 oz.) pkg. dark chocolate or semi-sweet chocolate chips

1 T. shortening

Colored candy sprinkles

Ribbons to match

Equipment

9" round baking pan, small cookie scoop, sheet of Styrofoam, white lollipop sticks

Preparation

Preheat oven to 325°. Coat pan with nonstick cooking spray. In a medium mixing bowl, beat the cream cheese at medium speed until smooth. Add sugar and flour; beat until light and fluffy. Reduce speed and add eggs; mix well. Mix in sour cream, vanilla extract and lemon juice until combined. Spread mixture in prepared pan. Set the pan in a hot water bath* and bake for approximately 40 minutes. Remove pan from water bath and cool cheesecake to room temperature. Cover and refrigerate for 3 hours or overnight.

When cheesecake is cold and firm, scoop out small balls from the pan. Roll with damp hands to shape smoothly. Heat candy melts (about 25 wafers) in the microwave until melted and smooth. Carefully insert a lollipop stick halfway into each cheesecake ball, pull it out and drizzle a little melted candy into each hole. Re-insert sticks. Freeze cheesecake pops for at least 1 hour.

Melt chocolate chips and shortening in the microwave until smooth. Spoon melted chocolate over each cheesecake pop, covering as much as desired. While chocolate is still wet, scatter candy sprinkles over the top. Push sticks into a sheet of Styrofoam until chocolate sets. Tie curly ribbon around each stick before serving. Pops may be refrigerated for a short time before serving if necessary.

* To make a hot water bath, set the baking pan in a larger roasting pan. Fill the roasting pan with boiling water until it reaches about halfway up the sides of the cake pan.

Serving Suggestions

✱ Cut a piece of Styrofoam to fit into a container, at least 3" deep. Cover foam with foil. Fill container with colored jellybeans and push ends of lollipop sticks into foam.

✱ Set cheesecake pops, with sticks up, in mini-cupcake liners or directly on a serving platter.

✱ Omit lollipop sticks. Using a small round cookie cutter (1¼ to 2"), cut out small disks of cheesecake.

Peppermint Brownie Pops

Makes about 2½ dozen

Brownies

6 oz. bittersweet baking chocolate

2 oz. unsweetened baking chocolate

¾ C. butter

1½ C. sugar

2½ tsp. vanilla extract

4 eggs

1 C. flour

¼ tsp. salt

1 T. crushed peppermint candy

¾ C. semi-sweet chocolate chips

Coating & Garnishes

12 squares vanilla-flavored almond bark

Additional crushed peppermint candy

Equipment

Brownie pops pan(s), white lollipop sticks or mini candy canes

Preparation

Preheat oven to 350°. Lightly coat pans with nonstick cooking spray. Set pan(s) on a cookie sheet for easy handling.

Melt bittersweet chocolate, unsweetened chocolate and butter in the microwave until smooth. Add sugar and vanilla extract, mixing until smooth. Stir in eggs, one at a time, until well mixed. Stir in flour and salt. Fold in candy and chocolate chips. Fill brownie pop molds about ¾ full. Bake 25 minutes

or until a few crumbs stick to a toothpick inserted into center of brownie pop. Place pan on cooling rack until nearly cool.

Carefully run a toothpick or butter knife around each brownie pop to loosen from pan, if needed. Invert pan to remove pops, applying gentle pressure to the bottom. Turn the brownies, flat side down, on waxed paper; insert sticks or candy canes from the top to within about ½" of the bottom of the pop. Cool completely.

In a small narrow bowl, melt three almond bark squares in the microwave until smooth. Place crushed peppermints in a small bowl. Lift the brownie pops carefully by the stick and dip into the melted bark, coating each pop about halfway. Immediately sprinkle with crushed candy. Set on waxed paper to dry. Working in batches, repeat with remaining brownie pops, almond bark and candy.

Variations

To create a variety of flavors, divide the brownie batter evenly between four small bowls. Stir one of the following into each bowl: ¾ teaspoon crushed peppermint candy, ¾ teaspoon instant coffee granules, 1–2 teaspoons toffee bits and 1–2 teaspoons crushed nuts. Bake as directed and dip pops into any pleasing combination of the following: melted chocolate- or vanilla-flavored almond bark followed by crushed peppermint candy, crushed toffee bits, crushed nuts or chocolate sprinkles.

Milk Chocolate Malt Cheesecakes

Makes 3 to 3½ dozen

Crust

½ C. finely crushed chocolate graham cracker crumbs

2¼ tsp. melted butter

Filling

¼ C. heavy or whipping cream

¼ C. malted milk powder

1 C. milk chocolate chips

2 (8 oz.) pkgs. cream cheese, softened

½ C. sugar

2 eggs

½ C. sour cream

1 tsp. vanilla extract

Topping & Garnish

2½ C. sweetened whipped cream or whipped topping

Milk chocolate shavings

Equipment

Nonstick mini muffin pan(s), optional plastic piping bag and tips

Preparation

Preheat oven to 350°. Coat muffin cups with nonstick cooking spray. In a small bowl, combine crumbs and butter. Spoon ½ to 1 teaspoon crumb mixture into each muffin cup; press firmly against bottom. Pour cream into a glass measuring cup and microwave for 40 seconds or until very warm. Stir in malt powder to dissolve. Let mixture stand for 5 to 10 minutes and then strain the cream. Melt chocolate chips in microwave and stir until smooth; set aside. In a medium mixing bowl, beat cream cheese at medium speed until smooth. Add sugar and mix well. Reduce speed and add eggs; beat until blended. Mix in sour cream and vanilla extract. Stir in strained cream. Mix in chocolate. Spoon batter into prepared pan over crusts, filling cups about ¾ full. Bake for 14 to 16 minutes or until set. Cool completely. Cover and refrigerate for 4 to 6 hours. Remove cheesecakes from pan. Pipe or place a dollop of whipped cream or topping on each cheesecake and garnish with shaved milk chocolate.

Surprise Brownie Babies

Makes about 2 dozen

Brownies

3 oz. unsweetened baking chocolate, chopped

⅓ C. butter

1 C. sugar

2 eggs, lightly beaten

1 tsp. vanilla extract

½ C. flour

Surprise Centers

24 Hershey's Hugs candies

Equipment

Nonstick mini muffin pan(s), mini cupcake liners

Preparation

Preheat oven to 350°. Insert liners in pans; set aside. Melt chocolate and butter in the microwave until smooth. Add sugar, eggs and vanilla extract; beat lightly until just combined. Stir in flour. Spoon about 1 tablespoon of batter into each muffin cup. Press one unwrapped candy into the center of each brownie.

Bake for 13 to 17 minutes or until a toothpick inserted between the candy and the edge of the pan comes out with a little batter. The brownies will continue to bake after they are removed from the oven. Let cool and decorate, if desired, with a sprinkling of powdered sugar or with one of the frostings on other pages of this book.

Variations

Try these different surprise centers: mini peanut butter cups, maraschino cherries, or mini candy bars. When available, try holiday-themed candy.

Orange-Kissed Brownie Wedges

Makes 1½ to 3 dozen

Brownies

2 eggs

1 C. sugar

⅔ C. flour

½ C. unsweetened cocoa powder

½ C. butter, melted

Frosting & Glaze

2 T. butter, softened

½ tsp. finely shredded orange peel

1¾ C. powdered sugar, divided

1 to 1½ T. orange juice, divided

Orange food coloring

2 oz. semi-sweet baking chocolate

¼ C. butter

Equipment

3 (4") nonstick springform pans

Preparation

Preheat oven to 350°. Lightly coat pans with nonstick cooking spray; set aside. In a medium mixing bowl, combine eggs and sugar. Beat at medium speed for 3 to 5 minutes or until thickened. Add flour and cocoa to egg mixture, beating just until smooth. Stir in melted butter until combined. Divide batter evenly between prepared pans. Bake for 25 to 30 minutes or until brownies test done. Cool completely in pans.

In a large mixing bowl, combine softened butter and orange peel. Add ½ cup powdered sugar and ½ tablespoon orange juice; beat on medium speed until blended. Beat in remaining 1¼ cups powdered sugar and enough orange juice to make a spreading consistency. Stir in food coloring. Spread frosting on cooled brownies in pans. Cover and chill 30 minutes.

Melt chocolate and ¼ cup butter in microwave until smooth. Cool 15 minutes. Spread chocolate over brownies. Chill 30 minutes to set glaze.

Remove brownies from pans. Cut into 6 to 8 wedges before serving.

Cranberry Blondies

Makes 3 to 5 dozen

Blondies

¾ C. butter, melted

1½ C. brown sugar

2 eggs

¾ tsp. vanilla extract

2¼ C. flour

1½ tsp. baking powder

¼ tsp. salt

⅛ tsp. ground cinnamon

½ C. dried cranberries

1 C. white baking chips

Frosting & Garnish

1 (8 oz.) pkg. cream cheese, softened

1 C. powdered sugar, sifted

1 T. grated orange peel

6 oz. white baking chocolate, melted

½ C. chopped dried cranberries

Equipment

9" x 13" nonstick baking pan

Preparation

Preheat oven to 350°. Coat pan with nonstick cooking spray. In a large bowl, combine butter and brown sugar; cool to room temperature. Beat in eggs and vanilla. In a small bowl, combine flour, baking powder, salt and cinnamon; gradually add to butter mixture. Stir in ½ cup cranberries and white baking chips. Spread batter in prepared pan and bake for 18 to 21 minutes or until blondies test done; cool.

In a medium mixing bowl, beat cream cheese until smooth. Mix in powdered sugar and orange peel. Gradually add half the melted chocolate, beating until blended. Spread frosting over blondies. Cut into small rectangles or squares. Sprinkle with chopped cranberries and drizzle with remaining melted chocolate. Immediately remove from pan. Store in refrigerator.

Variation

Use chopped dried apricots in place of the cranberries to make Apricot Blondies.

Chocolate & Mint Cheesecake Bites

Makes about 1½ dozen

Crust

1 C. finely crushed chocolate wafer crumbs

2 T. margarine, melted

2 T. sugar

Filling

2 (8 oz.) pkgs. cream cheese, softened

¾ C. sugar

2 eggs

½ tsp. vanilla or mint extract

⅓ C. mint (green) baking chips, melted

Green food coloring

⅓ C. dark chocolate and mint chips, chopped

Topping & Garnish

1 C. chocolate chips melted with
1 tsp. shortening

Andes mints, broken

Equipment

Nonstick mini cheesecake pan(s)

Preparation

In a small bowl, stir together crumbs, margarine and sugar. Divide mixture between cheesecake cups, using about 2 teaspoons per cup*. Pat crumbs into bottom of cups.

In a medium mixing bowl, beat cream cheese until smooth. Beat in sugar. Reduce speed and add eggs, mixing well. Stir in extract. Divide batter between two bowls. Stir melted mint chips and green food coloring into one bowl. Spoon green mixture into 8 cups in prepared pan, filling almost to the top. Stir chopped chocolate/mint chips into remaining batter. Spoon white mixture into remaining cups. Bake for 17 minutes or until set. Remove from oven and cool completely. Remove cheesecakes from pan(s). Before serving, spoon chocolate topping on each cheesecake and garnish with mint pieces.

If using just one mini cheesecake pan, reserve enough crumb mixture for a second batch of 4 to 6 cheesecakes. Chocolate wafer wedges can also be used as a garnish.

Bon Bon Delights

Makes 60 pieces

Filling

½ C. butter, softened

2 C. creamy peanut butter

1 tsp. vanilla extract

4 C. powdered sugar

3 C. crisp rice cereal

Coating & Garnishes

2½ C. semi-sweet or milk chocolate chips

2 T. shortening

Finely chopped peanuts or chocolate chips, optional

Preparation

For filling, in a large bowl, cream together butter, peanut butter and vanilla until blended. Mix in powdered sugar and cereal until well combined, using hands as needed. Using a small cookie scoop or hands, shape mixture into small, even balls. Place on a waxed paper-lined baking sheet and chill thoroughly.

For chocolate coating, place chocolate chips and shortening in a medium microwave-safe bowl. Microwave in 60-second intervals until melted and smooth, stirring often. Dip chilled balls into melted chocolate until coated, removing them with a fork and tapping it gently on the edge of the bowl to allow excess chocolate to drip off. Set on waxed paper. If desired, garnish with chopped nuts or chocolate chips while coating is still wet, or drizzle with remaining melted chocolate, reheating as needed. Refrigerate bon bons for several hours before serving or storing.

Peanut Butter Cheesecake Pops

Makes 2 to 3 dozen

Crust

1 C. finely crushed chocolate wafer cookie crumbs

⅓ C. peanuts, finely chopped

2 T. margarine, melted

Filling

2 (8 oz.) pkgs. cream cheese, softened

½ C. peanut butter

⅔ C. sugar

4 tsp. flour

½ tsp. vanilla extract

1 egg

1 egg yolk

2 T. heavy cream or half & half

Coating & Garnishes

20 to 24 oz. chocolate-flavored almond bark*

Chopped peanuts, crushed mini M&M baking bits, mini chocolate chips or crushed cookies

Equipment

8" x 8" baking pan, white lollipop sticks

* For a darker chocolate coating, dip cubes in a mixture of 1 cup chocolate chips (semi-sweet or dark chocolate) melted with 1 to 2 teaspoons shortening.

Preparation

Preheat oven to 375°. Line pan with foil, pressing bottom and sides as flat and smooth as possible. Coat foil with nonstick cooking spray. In a medium bowl, stir together cookie crumbs, peanuts and margarine. Press mixture into the bottom of prepared baking pan; set aside.

In a large mixing bowl, beat cream cheese at medium speed until smooth, about 30 seconds. Beat in peanut butter. Add sugar, flour and vanilla extract and beat until smooth. Reduce speed, add egg and egg yolk, and beat until well blended. Stir in cream. Pour filling mixture over crust in prepared pan. Place the pan in a larger pan and pour boiling water into the large pan until it comes halfway up the sides of the 8" pan. Bake for 40 minutes, then turn off oven and leave cheesecake there for 5 more minutes. Remove cheesecake from water and place on cooling rack. When completely cool, refrigerate for at least 4 hours or overnight.

To make pops, remove cheesecake from pan by lifting up on foil. Peel off foil. Cut cheesecake into small cubes with a long sharp knife, about 1" on all sides. Push a lollipop stick into the top of each cube and return to the refrigerator or freezer to chill well.

Meanwhile, in a narrow microwave-safe mug, melt 6 ounces of chocolate almond bark* and stir until smooth (for one batch). Arrange chopped nuts, candies or crumbs on small plates for dipping. Holding a cheesecake cube by the stick, dip the end into melted bark, pressing it down until the bark just coats the upper edges. Remove and let excess bark drip off. Dip bottom into desired garnishes and set on waxed paper to dry. Coat six more cubes, spooning bark over top edges as necessary. Repeat with additional batches of almond bark, melting 6 ounces (3 cubes) of bark for each batch of pops.

Variation

To serve an assortment of peanut butter cheesecakes on one platter, omit sticks on some cubes and leave them uncoated. Put sticks into remaining cubes and dip them in a variety of chocolate coatings and garnishes. If desired, stir miniature chocolate chips or chopped Reese's Peanut Butter Cups into the batter before baking.

Raspberry Swirl Cheesecake Cubes

Makes about 2 dozen

Crust

½ C. butter, softened

⅔ C. powdered sugar

¼ tsp. salt

1 C. flour

Filling

1 (4 oz.) bar white baking chocolate

1 C. fresh or frozen raspberries

1T water

2 (8 oz.) pkgs. cream cheese, softened

½ C. sugar

2 eggs

½ C. sour cream

1 tsp. vanilla extract

Red food coloring

¼ tsp. raspberry extract

Garnishes

½ C. white baking or dark chocolate chips

½ tsp. vegetable oil

Whipped topping and berries, optional

Equipment

8" x 8" baking pan, plastic bag for piping

Preparation

Preheat oven to 325°. Line pan with foil, allowing foil to extend about 2" over pan on all edges. In a medium mixing bowl, beat butter at medium-high speed until creamy. Add powdered sugar and salt; beat 1 minute until light and fluffy. Reduce speed and gradually beat in flour. Press mixture over bottom of prepared pan. Bake for about 18 minutes or until golden brown. Let crust cool on a wire rack.

To make filling, melt white baking chocolate in the microwave until smooth. Set aside to cool to room temperature. Meanwhile, combine raspberries and 1 tablespoon water in a microwave-safe bowl and microwave for 1 minute. Press through a strainer set over a bowl to get ¼ cup puree; discard seeds. In a large mixing bowl, beat together cream cheese and sugar at medium-high speed for 2 minutes. Reduce speed and beat in eggs until blended. Beat in sour cream and vanilla.

To raspberry puree, add 1 cup batter, food coloring and raspberry extract; mix well. Remove and reserve ½ cup of mixture. Whisk melted baking chocolate into remaining batter. Pour 1½ cups white batter over cooled crust. Top with spoonfuls of remaining raspberry mixture, then remaining white batter to cover. Top with dollops of reserved raspberry mixture. Drag a toothpick through layers to marbleize. Bake for about 1 hour, until slightly puffed and set. Cool completely, then refrigerate for 1 hour or overnight, until firm.

To serve, lift foil and cheesecake from pan and peel off foil. With a long sharp knife, cut cheesecake into 1⅛" cubes. Melt white or chocolate chips with oil in the microwave until smooth. Spoon mixture into a plastic bag and cut a tiny piece off one corner for piping. Drizzle lines of chocolate back and forth over the top of each cube. Set cheesecake cubes in miniature paper or foil cupcake liners. Garnish pieces with a dollop of whipped topping and a fresh blueberry or raspberry, if desired. Frilled toothpicks can be used for serving.

Double-Dipped Blondie Pops

Makes about 2 dozen

Blondies

6 oz. white baking chocolate, broken into pieces

1½ C. flour

½ tsp. baking powder

¼ tsp. salt

¾ C. sugar

2 eggs

2 T. water

⅛ tsp. almond extract

⅓ C. butter, melted and cooled

Coatings & Garnishes

6 oz. vanilla-flavored almond bark

6 oz. chocolate-flavored almond bark

6 oz. caramel bits or caramels

water

Crushed peanuts

Crushed toffee bits

Decorator sprinkles or nonpareils

Equipment

9" x 9" nonstick baking pan, white lollipop sticks

Preparation

Melt white baking chocolate in the microwave until smooth; cool to room temperature. Preheat oven to 350°. Lightly coat pan with nonstick cooking spray. In a small bowl, combine flour, baking powder and salt. In a large bowl, combine sugar, eggs, 2 tablespoons water and almond extract. To the large bowl, add melted chocolate and butter; stir until smooth. Gradually stir in flour mixture and pour into prepared pan. Bake for 24 to 30 minutes or until blondies test done. Let pan cool slightly until easy to handle but still warm.

Cut away hard outer edges, and then cut blondies into about 25 squares. Remove from pan and roll each square into a ball. Add a lollipop stick to each and refrigerate.

Place peanuts, toffee bits and sprinkles in three separate small bowls. In separate microwave-safe bowls, place vanilla bark, chocolate bark and caramel bits, adding water to the caramel as directed on package to make a very thin sauce. Working with one flavor of coating at a time, melt it in the microwave until smooth. Dip pops into a melted coating and immediately dip bottom of each pop into one of the garnishes. Reheat coating as needed to maintain a workable consistency. Allow coated pops to dry upright on waxed paper.

Make an assortment of blondie pops by applying a variety of coatings and garnishes in different ways:

Variations

✳ Dip some pops in a single coating and cover completely with finely crushed garnishes.

✳ Add food coloring to vanilla bark to make a variety of colors.

✳ Coat some pops in two or three different colors or flavors of coatings. Be sure to let the first coat dry before dipping again. Overlap layers as shown in photo.

Dainty Mocha Cheesecake Baskets

Makes about 2 dozen

Crust

½ C. finely crushed graham cracker crumbs

1 tsp. cocoa powder

24 square wonton wrappers

Filling

1 C. semi-sweet chocolate chips

1 C. heavy or whipping cream

1 (8 oz.) pkg. cream cheese, softened

2½ T. butter, softened

2½ T. coffee flavored liqueur
(such as Kahlua)*

1 tsp. vanilla extract

Garnishes

Fresh raspberries or strawberries

Chocolate curls or chocolate-covered
coffee beans

Equipment

Nonstick mini muffin or mini
cheesecake pan(s)

Preparation

Preheat oven to 400°. Coat 24 muffin cups with nonstick cooking spray. In a small bowl, stir together crumbs and cocoa powder. Place wonton wrappers on waxed paper; spray both sides with cooking spray. Sprinkle both sides with crumbs. Place a wrapper in each cup and press down gently until it molds into the cup and tips fan out. (Fill any empty cups in the pan with water to prevent warping.) Bake for 6 to 7 minutes or until golden brown. Cool 15 minutes before removing wonton baskets.

Melt chocolate chips in microwave until smooth. In a small chilled mixing bowl, beat cream at high speed until soft peaks form; set aside. In a medium mixing bowl, beat together cream cheese and butter. Add liqueur, vanilla and chocolate, mixing well. Fold in whipped cream until blended. Spoon filling into wonton baskets and chill for 30 minutes. Garnish as desired before serving.

* For a non-alcoholic substitute, dissolve ½ to 1 teaspoon instant coffee in 2 tablespoons water.

No-Bake Mandarin Orange Tartlets

Makes about 2 dozen

Filling

1 (8 oz.) pkg. cream cheese, softened

½ C. sugar

2 T. frozen orange juice concentrate, thawed

1 tsp. orange extract

½ (8 oz.) container extra-creamy whipped topping, thawed

1 tsp. grated orange peel

Crust & Garnish

24 baked mini Phyllo shells

Additional grated orange peel

Preparation

In a medium mixing bowl, beat cream cheese at medium speed until smooth. Add sugar and beat until light and fluffy. Beat in orange concentrate and orange extract. Fold in whipped topping and 1 teaspoon orange peel until well blended. Spoon a small amount of orange filling into each Phyllo shell and garnish with a sprinkling of additional orange peel. Cover and chill for 30 minutes.

Variations

Mix and match the fillings and shells on these two pages. Change the flavor of the wonton baskets in the previous recipe by replacing the cocoa powder in the crust mixture with ground cinnamon. Garnish each tartlet or basket with small pieces of fruit.

Tantalizing Truffles

Makes 42 pieces

Ingredients

¾ C. butter

1 C. peanut butter chips

½ C. unsweetened cocoa powder

1 (14 oz.) can sweetened condensed milk

1 T. vanilla extract

Additional cocoa powder, finely chopped peanuts, graham cracker crumbs, melted white or milk chocolate, optional

Preparation

In a large saucepan over low heat, melt butter and peanut butter chips, stirring often. Add ½ cup cocoa powder and stir until smooth. Stir in milk until blended. Cook for 4 minutes, stirring constantly, until mixture is thick and glossy. Remove from heat; stir in vanilla. Refrigerate for 2 hours or until firm enough to handle. Shape mixture into 1" balls. Roll balls in cocoa powder, nuts or graham cracker crumbs until coated. Balls may also be dipped or drizzled in melted chocolate. Refrigerate until firm, about 1 hour. Cover and store in refrigerator.

Fudge Jewels

Makes 36 pieces

Ingredients

3 C. sugar

¾ C. butter

1 (5 oz.) can evaporated milk

1 (12 oz.) pkg. white baking chips

1 (7 oz.) jar marshmallow creme

½ C. coarsely chopped Oreos

1 tsp. vanilla extract

Preparation

Line a 9" square baking pan with foil. Lightly coat foil with nonstick cooking spray; set aside. In a medium saucepan over medium heat, combine sugar, butter and milk. Bring to a full rolling boil for 3 minutes, stirring constantly. Remove from heat. Stir in baking chips, marshmallow creme, chopped Oreos and vanilla. Stir until chips are melted and mixture is smooth. Pour into prepared pan. Refrigerate for 1 hour or until firm. Using foil, lift fudge from pan. Remove foil before slicing into small pieces.

Triple Chocolate Cheesecake Wedges

Makes 2½ to 3 dozen

Crust

2 C. crushed cream-filled chocolate sandwich cookies (such as Oreos)

2 T. butter, melted

Filling

2 (8 oz.) pkgs. cream cheese, softened

½ C. sugar

1 T. flour

½ tsp. vanilla extract

4 (1 oz.) squares semi-sweet baking chocolate, melted and cooled

2 eggs

Coating

Chocolate-flavored almond bark (6 oz. will coat 8 wedges)

Vanilla-flavored almond bark (6 oz. will coat 8 wedges)

Sparkle gel (red, green)

2 oz. vanilla-flavored almond bark (for drizzling)

Equipment

4 (4") nonstick springform pans, white lollipop sticks

Preparation

Preheat oven to 325°. In a medium bowl, stir together cookie crumbs and melted butter. Lightly coat pans with nonstick cooking spray. Press ½ cup of crumb mixture into the bottom of each springform pan; set aside. In a medium mixing bowl, beat cream cheese at medium speed just until smooth. Add sugar, flour and vanilla; beat until well combined. Mix in melted chocolate. Reduce speed and add eggs, mixing until blended. Pour ¼ of filling over each crust, smoothing tops. Set springform pans on a baking sheet with edges. Bake for 38 to 41 minutes or until set. Cool completely, then refrigerate for 4 hours or overnight.

Remove cheesecake from pan. Cut each cheesecake into eight wedges. Push a lollipop stick into the end of each wedge and refrigerate for at least 30 minutes.

Melt 6 ounces of almond bark in the microwave following package instructions; stir until smooth. Holding a cheesecake wedge on a fork over the bowl, spoon melted bark over the top and sides; tap fork lightly against bowl to let excess bark drip off. Place on waxed paper to dry. Repeat with remaining bark and wedges. Top with sparkle gel and additional almond bark, as desired.

Variations

To create a party platter, prepare crust and filling as directed. Make two plain chocolate pans. Then use the ideas below to create one pan of peppermint and one raspberry. Garnish wedges from each pan differently, coating some in chocolate, some in vanilla and leaving others uncoated. Drizzle with contrasting bark or gels and arrange wedges on a round platter with points meeting in the middle.

Peppermint Cheesecake

Crush a candy cane and sprinkle over one crust before adding filling. After baking, chilling and slicing, coat wedges in chocolate almond bark and sprinkle additional crushed candy on top while bark is wet.

Raspberry Cheesecake

Spread 1 tablespoon raspberry preserves over center of one crust before adding filling. After baking, chilling and slicing, coat wedges in vanilla almond bark and drizzle sparkle gel over top as desired.

CAKE POPS, CUPCAKES & OTHER PETITE SWEETS

Brownie Bomb Pops

Makes about 2½ dozen

Brownies

1 (1 oz.) square unsweetened chocolate

1 (3 oz.) pkg. cream cheese, softened

¼ C. butter, softened

¾ C. sugar

2 eggs

⅔ C. flour

½ tsp. baking powder

¼ tsp. salt

Powdered Sugar Icing

2 C. sifted powdered sugar

1 to 2 T. milk

¼ tsp. vanilla extract

Food coloring of choice, optional

Garnish

Nonpareils

Equipment

9" x 9" baking pan, parchment paper, white cookie sticks, colored drinking straws

Preparation

Preheat oven to 350°. Line pan with parchment paper, allowing 2" to hang over all sides of pan. Melt unsweetened chocolate in the microwave until smooth; cool. In a medium mixing bowl, beat cream cheese at medium speed until smooth. Add butter and sugar; mix until smooth. Beat in eggs. In a small bowl, combine flour, baking powder and salt; stir into creamed mixture. Add cooled chocolate; stir to combine. Pour into prepared pan. Bake for 15 to 20 minutes; cool in pan.

Gripping parchment paper, remove cooled brownies from pan. Cut into bars about 1" wide and 2" long. Insert a cookie stick into one end of each brownie as far as possible without pushing stick through to the other side.

Mix powdered sugar, milk, vanilla and food coloring, if desired, until smooth and of drizzling consistency. Drizzle icing over three sides of the bomb pops and the end opposite the stick, leaving about ½" unfrosted near the stick. Sprinkle with nonpareils. Set on a cooling rack or waxed paper until dry. Drizzle icing over the uncoated side to within ½" of stick, sprinkle with nonpareils and let dry. Slide drinking straw over stick and trim to same length.

Variations

Checkerboard Brownie Bomb Pops

Prepare batter as directed, setting aside the melted and cooled chocolate. Drop half the plain batter from a tablespoon, checkerboard fashion, into prepared pan. To remaining batter in bowl, stir in chocolate. Drop chocolate batter from tablespoon into open spaces in pan. Bake and decorate as directed.

Checkerboard Mint Brownie Bomb Pops

Prepare batter as directed, setting aside the melted and cooled chocolate. Divide batter between two bowls. To one bowl, stir in chocolate. To remaining bowl, add ½ teaspoon peppermint extract and several drops of green food coloring; stir well. Drop half the chocolate batter from a tablespoon, checkerboard fashion, into prepared pan. Drop peppermint batter from tablespoon into open spaces in pan. Bake and decorate as directed.

Chocolate-Covered Cherry Cheesecake Bits

Makes about 3 dozen

Filling

2 (8 oz.) pkgs. cream cheese, softened

⅓ C. sugar

⅓ C. sour cream

1 tsp. vanilla extract

2 eggs

¼ C. finely crushed gingersnap cookie crumbs

1 (22 oz.) can cherry pie filling, divided

Coating

1½ C. bittersweet, semi-sweet or milk chocolate chips

2 T. shortening

Equipment

8" x 8" baking pan, mini paper or mini foil cupcake liners, optional

Preparation

Preheat oven to 350°. Line pan with foil and coat with nonstick cooking spray. In a medium mixing bowl, beat cream cheese at medium speed until smooth. Beat in sugar gradually. Add sour cream and vanilla; beat until blended. Reduce speed and add eggs, beating until smooth. Fold in crumbs and spread mixture in prepared pan. Bake 40 minutes or until set and lightly browned. Cool for 40 minutes and then refrigerate for at least 2 hours.

Lift foil and cheesecake from pan. Cut off edges to level the top. Lightly score cheesecake into small squares. Press the end of a wooden spoon into the middle of each square, about ¼" deep. Mash the cherries from half of the pie filling and spread over cheesecake. Freeze for 1 hour.

Cut cheesecake as scored and remove from pan. Melt chocolate chips and shortening in the microwave until smooth. Holding a cheesecake square on a fork over the bowl, spoon chocolate over square until coated; tap fork to let excess chocolate drip off. Set on waxed paper to dry. If desired, garnish with remaining pie filling before serving in paper or foil liners.

No-Bake Pumpkin Wedges

Makes about 2 dozen

Crust

1½ C. finely crushed gingersnap cookie crumbs

3 T. butter, melted

Filling

1 (1 lb., 8.3 oz.) tub refrigerated cheesecake filling

½ (15 oz.) can pumpkin puree

¾ tsp. pumpkin pie spice

Garnishes

Whipped topping

Ground cinnamon or gingersnap crumbs

Toasted pecan halves, optional

Equipment

4 (4") nonstick springform pans

Preparation

Lightly coat pans with nonstick cooking spray. In a small bowl, stir together crumbs and butter. Divide mixture evenly among four (4") springform pans and press firmly into bottom of pans. Bake crust for 7 minutes; cool completely.

Stir cheesecake filling until smooth. Transfer half of the filling to a medium bowl; set aside. Divide and spread remaining filling evenly over the crusts in the springform pans. To filling in the bowl, add pumpkin puree and spice; mix well. Divide and spread pumpkin filling evenly over the plain cheesecake in each pan. Cover and refrigerate at least 4 hours or until set.

To serve, remove pan sides. Cut each cheesecake into six or eight wedges and transfer to a serving platter. Garnish wedges with a dollop of whipped topping and a sprinkling of cinnamon or gingersnap crumbs; add a toasted pecan, if desired.

Strawberry Cheesecake Minis

Makes 1½ to 2 dozen

Crust

1¼ C. finely crushed vanilla wafer crumbs

2 T. sugar

1½ T. butter, melted

Filling

2 (8 oz.) pkgs. cream cheese, softened

½ C. sugar

½ tsp. vanilla extract

½ tsp. strawberry flavoring

2 eggs

¼ C. strawberry preserves

Red food coloring

Garnishes

Whipped topping (plain or strawberry-flavored)

Chocolate filigrees (Refer to instructions on page 118.)

Equipment

Nonstick mini cheesecake pan(s), plastic bags

Preparation

Preheat oven to 350°. In a small bowl, stir together crumbs, sugar and melted butter. Firmly press approximately 1 tablespoon of crumb mixture into the bottom of each cheesecake cup; set aside. In a medium mixing bowl, beat cream cheese at medium speed until smooth. Beat in sugar, vanilla and strawberry flavoring. Reduce speed and add eggs, mixing until well blended. Stir in preserves and food coloring to reach desired color. Spoon cheesecake mixture into prepared pan, filling each cup about ⅔ full. Bake for 15 to 18 minutes or until set. Cool completely. Refrigerate 3 hours or overnight. Remove cheesecakes from pan and garnish with a dollop of whipped topping and a chocolate filigree. (For help making filigrees, see page 118.)

Variation

Make Raspberry Cheesecake Minis by using seedless raspberry preserves and flavoring in place of strawberry preserves and flavoring. Garnish with fresh raspberries.

Rainbow Blondie Party Pops

Makes about 1½ dozen

Blondies

½ C. butter, softened

¾ C. brown sugar

1 egg white

½ tsp. vanilla extract

1 C. flour

¼ tsp. baking soda

1 C. mini M&M baking bits

½ C. chopped pecans

Coating & Garnishes

2 C. white baking chips

1 T. shortening

Nonpareils or mini baking bits (partially crushed, if desired)

Equipment

8" x 8" baking pan, parchment paper, wooden popsicle sticks

Preparation

Preheat oven to 350°. Line pan with parchment paper, allowing 2" to hang over all sides of pan. In a medium mixing bowl, cream butter and sugar on medium speed until light and fluffy. Beat in egg and vanilla. In a small bowl, combine flour and baking soda; add to creamed mixture just until combined. Dough will be stiff. Stir in baking bits and pecans. Spread dough in prepared pan. Bake for 20 to 30 minutes or until blondies test nearly done. Cool completely.

Gripping parchment paper, remove blondies from pan. Cut into 16 squares. Insert a popsicle stick into one cut edge of each square; chill.

Melt white baking chips and shortening in the microwave until smooth. Holding a blondie on a fork over the bowl, spoon melted coating over the top and sides; tap fork lightly against bowl to smooth coating and let excess drip off. Sprinkle with nonpareils or baking bits while wet. Place on cooling rack or waxed paper until coating has set. If desired, carefully coat the bottom of each blondie pop after top and sides are dry.

Cookie Crust Cheesecakes

Cherry-Topped Cheesecakes
Makes about 4 dozen

Crust

Small vanilla wafers (or cookies of choice as listed in the Variations.)

Filling

2 (8 oz.) pkgs. cream cheese, softened

½ C. sugar

1 tsp. vanilla extract

2 eggs

Topping

Cherry pie filling

Equipment

Nonstick mini muffin pan(s), mini cupcake liners

Preparation

Preheat oven to 325°. Place liner in each muffin cup and set a wafer in the bottom of each liner. In a medium mixing bowl, beat cream cheese at medium speed until smooth. Beat in sugar and vanilla. Reduce speed and add eggs, beating until blended. Spoon approximately 1 tablespoon of filling over each wafer, filling liners about ¾ full. Bake for 15 to 18 minutes or until set. Let cool completely. Chill for at least 1 hour. Just before serving, top each cheesecake with a small amount of pie filling.

Variations

To serve a whole platter of mini-cheesecakes in a variety of flavors, use the suggestions below to vary the liner flavors as desired. Then make the basic cheesecake filling. Divide the mixture between six bowls (or the number of flavor combinations you wish to make). Stir in a small amount of any of the ingredients that follow in any combinations you like. Garnish as desired. Note: The amounts given for each variation are for making a whole batch of that particular flavor.

Chocolate Chip Cheesecakes

Use small chocolate chip cookies in liners. Add ¾ cup miniature chocolate chips to filling mixture, fill cups and bake as directed. Drizzle with fudge sauce.

Oreo Cheesecakes

Prop small Oreo cookies on edge in liners. Add ¾ cup crushed Oreo cookies to filling mixture, fill cups and bake as directed. Garnish with whipped topping and crushed cookies.

Peanut Butter Cheesecakes

Use small Nutter Butter cookies in liners. Add ½ cup creamy peanut butter to filling mixture, fill cups and bake as directed. Garnish with fudge sauce or cookie crumbles.

Chocolate Cheesecakes

Use Oreo Thin Crisps in liners. Add ¼ cup unsweetened cocoa powder to filling mixture, fill cups and bake as directed. Garnish with fudge sauce and cookie sprinkles.

Spice Cheesecakes

Use small gingersnaps in liners. Add 2 teaspoons pumpkin pie spice or ground cinnamon to filling mixture, fill cups and bake as directed. Garnish with whipped topping and finely crushed gingersnaps or ground cinnamon.

Lime Cheesecake Mini Tarts

Makes about 6 dozen

Crust

4 oz. cream cheese, softened

1 egg

1 T. fresh lime juice

½ C. butter, melted

1 (18.25 oz.) box French vanilla cake mix

White baking chips

Filling

1 (24.3 oz.) tub prepared lime cheesecake filling*

½ to 1 tsp. finely grated lime peel, optional

Garnishes

Finely shredded lime peel

Dark or semi-sweet chocolate chips, chopped, optional

Chocolate curls, optional

Equipment

Nonstick mini muffin pan(s)

Preparation

Preheat oven to 350°. In a medium mixing bowl, beat cream cheese at medium speed until smooth. Reduce speed and add egg, lime juice and butter; beat until combined, about 1 minute. Stir in cake mix with a spoon until well mixed and dough is thick and pliable. Press about 1½ teaspoons of dough into each muffin cup, pressing it up the sides to the top of each cup. Place several white baking chips in each cup. Bake for 6 to 8 minutes or until light golden brown. Cool crusts for 10 minutes before removing from baking pan. Cool completely before filling.

Just before serving, stir lime peel into cheesecake filling, if desired. Spoon or pipe filling into each crust. Garnish with a sprinkling of lime peel, chopped chocolate or chocolate curls as desired. (If filled tarts are refrigerated overnight, crusts will soften.)

* Fill these tarts with any no-bake cheesecake filling such as the mocha filling or mandarin orange filling on pages 26 and 27.

Variations

Mini Lime Cheesecake Wedges

Use one or more 4" springform pans. Prepare crust mixture as directed but omit the white chips. Press ⅓ cup of dough into the bottom of a 4" springform pan. (Use as many pans as desired.) Bake crust for 14 minutes or until lightly browned. Cool completely. Spread 1 cup of lime cheesecake filling over the crust and refrigerate for at least 2 hours or overnight before cutting into wedges to serve. Garnish wedges with a dollop of whipped topping and grated chocolate or a chocolate filigree heart as directed on page 118.

Lime Cheesecake Bites

Use mini muffin pans with paper or foil liners. Fit mini muffin pans with paper liners. Prepare crust mixture as directed, but omit the white chips. Press 1 teaspoon of dough into the bottom of each paper liner. Bake for 6 to 7 minutes or until lightly browned; cool completely. Before serving, mound lime cheesecake filling into each liner and garnish as desired.

Tiki Bar Volcanoes

Piña Colada
Makes 1½ dozen

Filling

2 (8 oz.) pkgs. cream cheese, softened

⅔ C. sugar

2 eggs

1 tsp. rum flavoring

¾ C. finely chopped dried pineapple

¾ C. toasted coconut*

Base & Toppings

1 C. white baking chips

1 T. shortening

16 to 18 coconut macaroon cookies**

Additional chopped, dried pineapple and toasted coconut

Equipment

Mini cheesecake pan(s)

Preparation

Preheat oven to 350°. Coat pan with nonstick cooking spray; set aside. In a medium mixing bowl, beat cream cheese at medium speed until smooth. Beat in sugar. Reduce speed and add eggs, beating until blended. Stir in flavoring, pineapple and coconut until well mixed. Spoon mixture into cheesecake cups, filling about ¾ full. Bake for 18 minutes or until set. Cool completely. Chill for at least 2 hours.

To assemble, remove cheesecakes from pans. Melt baking chips with shortening in the microwave until smooth. Fasten the bottom of each cheesecake to the top of a cookie with a little melted mixture. Drizzle white mixture over the top of each "volcano" and mound some chopped pineapple and coconut in the center while wet.

To toast, place coconut in a single layer on a baking sheet. Bake at 350° for 5 to 8 minutes or until coconut is golden brown.

*** Cookies can be purchased or homemade.*

Variations

To create a party platter, make three flavors from one batch of filling. Simply prepare the filling for Piña Colada flavor, but omit the rum flavoring. Divide the filling between three bowls and add reduced amounts of the required flavorings to each bowl. Bake, chill and garnish each flavor as directed. Note: The amounts given for each variation are for making a whole batch of that particular flavor.

Grasshopper

Make cheesecake as directed, but substitute ½ teaspoon mint flavoring for rum flavoring and add 2 teaspoons crème de menthe ice cream topping. Stir in green food coloring, if desired. Use chocolate wafers for the base in place of macaroons and drizzle melted white chips and fudge topping over the top. Sprinkle with chopped Andes candies.

Strawberry/Raspberry Daiquiri

Make cheesecake as directed, but in addition to rum flavoring, add 1 teaspoon lemon flavoring and 1 teaspoon strawberry or raspberry flavoring. Stir in red food coloring, if desired. Use oatmeal cookies for the base in place of macaroons and drizzle melted white chips and raspberry preserves over the top. Sprinkle with chopped oatmeal cookies.

Black & White Cut-Ups

Makes about 4 dozen

Brownies

1 (19.95 oz.) pkg. brownie mix, any variety

Water, eggs and oil as directed on package

Coatings

1 C. white baking chips

2 T. shortening, divided

1 C. semi-sweet chocolate chips

Equipment

9" x 13" baking pan, parchment paper, 1½" to 2" oval cookie cutter, white lollipop sticks

Preparation

Preheat oven to 325°. Line pan with parchment paper, allowing 2" to hang over all sides of pan. Combine brownie mix, water, eggs and oil as directed on package. Bake brownies according to directions. Let cool.

Gripping parchment paper, remove brownies from pan. Cut as many oval shapes from the brownies as possible, brushing off crumbs; move cut-outs to waxed paper. Carefully insert lollipop sticks into one cut side of each oval as far as possible. Push down slightly on the cutouts to help adhere to the stick.

Melt white baking chips and 1 tablespoon shortening in the microwave until smooth. Holding each oval by its stick above the bowl, carefully spoon the white mixture over half of the top and sides, allowing the excess to drip off. Repeat as needed until well-covered. Tap gently against the bowl to distribute coating evenly. Place on waxed paper until set. Melt chocolate chips and remaining 1 tablespoon shortening in the microwave until smooth. In the same manner, spoon melted chocolate over the uncoated parts of each oval until covered. Place on waxed paper until set.

Variation

Throw a football-themed party by decorating these brownie ovals in your favorite team's colors, using colored candy melts or tinted almond bark.

Triangle Treats

Makes 4 to 6 dozen

Brownies

1 (19.95 oz.) pkg. brownie mix, any variety

Water, eggs and oil as directed on package

Toppings

1 (16 oz.) container cream cheese frosting

¾ C. salted peanuts, coarsely chopped

1 C. creamy peanut butter

1 (12 oz.) pkg. semi-sweet chocolate chips

3 C. crisp rice cereal

Equipment

9" x 13" nonstick baking pan

Preparation

Preheat oven to 350°. Lightly coat pan with nonstick cooking spray. Combine brownie mix, water, eggs and oil as directed on package. Bake brownies according to package directions. Cool completely in pan. Frost brownies with cream cheese frosting; sprinkle with peanuts and refrigerate.

Melt peanut butter and chocolate chips in the microwave; stir until smooth. In a large bowl, combine cereal and peanut butter mixture; stir until evenly coated. Spread evenly over frosted bars. Refrigerate until set. Slice into triangle pieces by cutting rows 1¾" to 2" wide along the length and width of the pan, then cutting each square in half, diagonally. To make slicing easier, run a sharp knife under warm water and dry it off before slicing these brownie triangles.

Tiny Turtle Cheesecakes

Makes about 3 dozen

Crust

1 C. finely crushed graham cracker or Teddy Graham crumbs

1½ T. margarine, melted

Filling

2 (8 oz.) pkgs. cream cheese, softened

½ C. sugar

⅓ C. unsweetened cocoa powder

1 tsp. vanilla extract

2 eggs

Garnishes

36 pecan halves

¾ C. caramel bits

1½ to 2 tsp. water

Equipment

Nonstick mini muffin pan(s)

Preparation

Preheat oven to 350°. With a pastry brush or paper towel, coat muffin cups with melted margarine. Divide crumbs evenly among cups and gently shake pans to coat bottoms and sides with crumbs; set aside. In a medium mixing bowl, beat cream cheese at medium speed until smooth. Add sugar, cocoa and vanilla; beat until blended. Reduce speed and beat in eggs until well mixed. Spoon about 1 tablespoon of filling into each muffin cup, filling about ¾ full. Bake for 12 to 15 minutes or until set. Cool in pan for 15 minutes. Run a small knife around edge of each cup to loosen and lift out cheesecakes. Cool for 30 minutes on a wire rack. Cover and chill for at least 1 hour. Before serving, combine caramel bits with 1½ to 2 teaspoons water in a microwave-safe bowl. Cook in 30 second intervals, stirring until smooth and thick. Spoon caramel mixture on each cheesecake and top with a pecan half.

Blueberry Cheesecake Fudge Minis

Makes about 4 dozen

Cheesecake Fudge

⅔ C. evaporated milk

2½ C. sugar

5 oz. marshmallow creme

¼ C. butter

1 (3 oz.) pkg. cream cheese, cubed and softened

1 (12 oz.) pkg. vanilla baking chips

1 (4 oz.) pkg. dried blueberries (¾ C.)

1 tsp. vanilla extract

1 tsp. butter flavoring

Garnishes

Whipped topping

Fresh blueberries

Equipment

9" x 9" nonstick baking pan, mini cupcake liners

Preparation

Spray pan with nonstick cooking spray, then line the bottom with parchment paper, trimmed to fit. In a medium saucepan over medium heat, warm evaporated milk. Stir in sugar, and slowly bring mixture to a rolling boil, stirring constantly to prevent scorching. Stir in marshmallow creme and butter. Bring mixture back to a full boil and boil for 4½ minutes, stirring constantly. Add cream cheese to the boiling mixture and boil for 1 minute longer. Remove from heat and add baking chips and blueberries. Stir until all chips are melted and mixture is creamy. Stir in vanilla and butter flavoring until well blended. Pour mixture into prepared pan and cool completely before cutting.

To remove from pan, cut around edges of pan with a sharp knife to loosen fudge. Place a cutting board on top of pan and flip over on the board to pop fudge out of pan. Peel off parchment paper, leaving a smooth surface on top. Cut into 1⅛" squares with a sharp knife or crinkle-cut slicer, or cut out shapes with a small flower or round cookie cutter (1" to 1½") coated with nonstick cooking spray. Serve pieces in mini cupcake liners and garnish with whipped topping and blueberries, if desired.

German Chocolate Brownie Pops

Makes 1 to 1½ dozen

Brownies

½ C. butter, softened

1 (4 oz.) bar German's sweet chocolate, chopped

½ C. sugar

1 tsp. vanilla extract

2 eggs

1 C. flour

½ tsp. baking powder

¼ tsp. salt

Topping

2 T. butter

½ C. brown sugar

2 T. corn syrup

2 T. milk

1 C. toasted coconut*

½ C. finely chopped pecans or walnuts

Equipment

Nonstick mini cheesecake pan(s), wooden popsicle sticks

Variations

Milk Chocolate Brownie Pops

Omit the German chocolate topping and decorate brownie pops with melted milk chocolate chips and chocolate nonpareils or colored sprinkles.

Preparation

Preheat oven to 350°. Lightly coat pan with nonstick cooking spray. In a small saucepan over low heat, melt ½ cup butter and the chocolate, stirring constantly; cool slightly. Add sugar and vanilla; blend well. Add eggs and beat well. In a small bowl, combine flour, baking powder and salt; add to chocolate mixture, stirring well. Spoon batter into pan, filling each cup about ⅔ full. Bake for 14 to 17 minutes or until brownies test nearly done. Cool 5 minutes and then insert a popsicle stick into each brownie; cool completely. Remove brownies from pan by pushing up from the bottom. If they do not remove easily from pan, run a toothpick or small knife around the edges of each cup to loosen brownie.

In a small saucepan, melt 2 tablespoons butter; add brown sugar, syrup and milk and blend well. Stir in coconut and pecans. Cook until sugar dissolves and mixture is bubbly, stirring constantly. Remove from heat. While topping is still warm, use a damp knife to spread topping around the lower half of each brownie as shown in photo, lightly pressing topping in place; chill.

* To toast, place coconut in a single layer on a baking sheet. Bake at 350° for 5 to 8 minutes or until coconut is golden brown.

Quick Caramel Brownie Pops

Instead of making the boiled topping, melt caramels or caramel bits (with water as directed on package to make thinner consistency) in the microwave until smooth. Frost the sides of each brownie pop as instructed above and press the toasted coconut and nuts into the warm caramel.

Little Rocky Roads

Makes about 2½ dozen

Brownies

1 C. butter

2 C. semi-sweet chocolate chips

1 C. sugar

1 C. brown sugar

1 tsp. salt

4 eggs

1¼ C. flour

1 C. chopped walnuts

Topping

1 C. chopped walnuts

1 C. semi-sweet chocolate chips

1½ C. miniature marshmallows

Equipment

Nonstick mini cheesecake pan(s)

Preparation

Preheat oven to 350°. Coat pans with nonstick cooking spray. Melt butter and 2 cups chocolate chips in the microwave until smooth. Stir in sugar, brown sugar and salt. Add eggs and flour, stirring just until combined. Mix in 1 cup walnuts. Immediately spoon mixture into prepared pan, filling each cup about ½ full. Bake for 15 to 17 minutes or until brownies test nearly done. Remove from oven; sprinkle 1 teaspoon chopped walnuts, 1 teaspoon chocolate chips and 6 marshmallows on each brownie. Return to oven; bake until marshmallows are puffed and lightly browned, 5 to 6 minutes. Cool 5 to 10 minutes. Remove brownies from pan by pushing up from the bottom. If necessary, run a toothpick or small knife around each cup to loosen brownie.

Variation

To use a 9" x 13" pan instead, line it with foil and coat with nonstick cooking spray. Spread batter in pan and bake 30 minutes or until brownies test nearly done. Remove from oven and sprinkle with walnuts, chocolate chips and marshmallows. Bake until marshmallows are puffed and lightly browned, 5 to 6 minutes. Cool 5 to 10 minutes. Remove brownies from pan and cut into small pieces.

Cupcakes

Whether you are feeling angelic or devilish, nutty or kissable, the cupcakes in this chapter will sweeten your days. Go ahead and try them all. Then swap the cupcakes and toppings to make other perfect combinations. Below are some tips for making delicious cupcakes.

Cupcake Tips

✳ For best results, preheat the oven before baking cupcakes.

✳ Grease muffin cups or small ramekins, or line each cup with paper or foil liners. Spoon the batter into prepared cups, filling each cup ½ to ⅔ full.

✳ When baking a single pan of cupcakes, place the pan on the middle rack in the oven. Stagger multiple pans on racks so heat can circulate.

✳ When a recipe calls for cake flour, do not use the self-rising type. If cake flour is not available, sift all-purpose flour, measure 1 cup and then remove 2 tablespoons; this will be equal to 1 cup of cake flour. For lighter cakes, add 2 tablespoons of cornstarch to replace the 2 tablespoons of flour you removed. Sift again before using.

✳ To use your favorite cake recipes to make cupcakes, bake cupcakes at the same temperature as directed for cake, but shorten baking time by one-third to one-half. A recipe that makes a 2-layer cake will make 24 to 30 standard cupcakes. If making miniature or jumbo cupcakes, adjust baking time accordingly.

✳ Use the toothpick method to check the doneness on cupcakes made with butter, oil or shortening. A toothpick inserted in the center should come out clean. If the toothpick comes out wet, bake longer. For angel food, chiffon or sponge cupcakes, test doneness by touching tops lightly; they should spring back.

✳ Refrigerate cupcakes frosted with dairy products such as cream cheese or whipping cream if they won't be eaten promptly.

✳ Unfrosted cupcakes may be frozen in an airtight container and kept for several months. Thaw cupcakes before decorating.

Milky Way Sweetcakes

Makes about 18 standard cupcakes

Cupcakes

10 miniature Milky Way candy bars, unwrapped and chopped

¼ C. butter

1 C. white sugar

½ C. shortening

2 medium eggs

1¼ C. all-purpose flour

½ tsp. salt

¾ C. buttermilk

¼ tsp. baking soda

½ tsp. vanilla extract

Toppings

1 (16 oz.) can ready-to-spread chocolate frosting

Miniature semi-sweet chocolate chips

Chopped pecans

Caramel ice cream topping

Milk chocolate kiss candies, unwrapped

Preparation

Preheat oven to 350°. Grease 18 muffin tin cups or fit the cups with paper liners.

In a heavy saucepan over low heat, melt candy bars and butter, stirring until smooth; set aside. In a large mixing bowl, beat together sugar and shortening until creamy. Add eggs, beating just until blended; set aside. In a separate bowl, combine flour and salt; set aside. In a measuring cup, stir together buttermilk and baking soda. Gradually add flour and buttermilk mixtures alternately to sugar mixture. Beat at low speed after each addition, just until blended. Stir in melted candy bar mixture and vanilla. Spoon batter evenly into the muffin cups.

Bake the cupcakes for 18 minutes or until a toothpick inserted in the center comes out clean. Let the pans cool on a rack for 10 minutes before removing cupcakes from pans to cool completely.

Spread frosting on cupcakes. Sprinkle some chocolate chips and pecans on top. Drizzle with caramel topping. Add a piped dollop of frosting in the center and top with a chocolate kiss.

Carnival Poke Cupcakes

Makes about 24 standard cupcakes

Cupcakes

1 (18.25 oz.) box plain white cake mix

Eggs, oil and water as directed on box

1 (3 oz.) pkg. gelatin, any color or flavor

1 C. boiling water

Toppings

4 C. powdered sugar

½ C. butter, melted

1 T. clear vanilla extract

4 to 5 T. half & half

Food coloring

Additional powdered sugar

Preparation

Preheat oven to 350°. Grease 24 muffin tin cups or line the cups with paper liners.

In a large mixing bowl, combine cake mix with eggs, oil and water as directed on cake mix box. Mix as directed and spoon batter evenly into the muffin cups.

Bake as directed for cupcakes. Let the pans cool on a rack for 10 minutes. Meanwhile, place dry gelatin in a bowl and add boiling water; stir until dissolved and set aside. Pierce top of each cupcake several times with a fork. Spoon gelatin mixture over cupcakes. Refrigerate for 30 minutes.

Meanwhile, prepare the toppings. Combine 4 cups powdered sugar, butter, vanilla and enough half & half to make a thick drizzling consistency. Frost cupcakes with a smooth layer of icing, reserving ¾ cup icing. Divide reserved icing among four bowls; tint each with food coloring. Stir additional powdered sugar into each bowl to reach piping consistency. Transfer colored icings into separate plastic freezer bags, cut off a corner of each bag and pipe lines of icing on cupcakes as desired.

Luscious Lemonade Cupcakes

Makes about 30 standard cupcakes

Cupcakes

1 (6 oz.) can frozen lemonade concentrate, thawed

1 (18.25 oz.) box white cake mix

1 (8 oz.) carton sour cream

1 (3 oz.) pkg. cream cheese, softened

3 large eggs

Pink Lemonade Buttercream Frosting

½ C. vegetable shortening

½ C. butter, softened

2 to 3 T. lemon juice or remaining lemonade concentrate

1 tsp. grated lemon zest

4 C. powdered sugar

Additional lemon juice

Pink food coloring

Candied lemon slices or drops, optional

Preparation

Preheat oven to 350°. Grease 30 muffin tin cups or fit the cups with paper liners.

Remove 2 tablespoons of lemonade concentrate from can and reserve for frosting or another use. In a large mixing bowl, combine remaining concentrate, cake mix, sour cream, cream cheese and eggs; beat at low speed until moistened. Beat at high speed for 3 minutes. Spoon batter evenly into the muffin cups.

Bake the cupcakes for 22 minutes or until a toothpick inserted in the center comes out clean. Let the pans cool on a rack for 10 minutes before removing cupcakes from pans to cool completely.

Meanwhile, prepare the frosting. Cream together shortening and butter. Beat in 2 tablespoons lemon juice and zest. Add powdered sugar gradually and beat until light and fluffy, adding food coloring and additional lemon juice if needed. Frost cupcakes and garnish with candied lemon slices or drops.

Scrumptious Strawberry Cupcakes

Makes about 24 standard cupcakes

Cupcakes

2½ C. cake flour

1 tsp. baking soda

¼ tsp. salt

½ C. unsalted butter, softened

1½ C. white sugar

2 large eggs

⅓ C. buttermilk

¼ C. canola oil

1 tsp. vanilla extract

1 C. finely chopped fresh or frozen strawberries

Strawberry Frosting

1 C. butter

3½ C. powdered sugar

½ tsp. vanilla extract

½ C. frozen strawberries, thawed and pureed

Fresh strawberries

Preparation

Preheat oven to 350°. Grease 24 muffin tin cups or fit the cups with paper liners.

In a medium bowl, whisk together flour, baking soda and salt; set aside. In a large mixing bowl, cream together butter and sugar. Add eggs, beating until smooth and creamy. Mix in buttermilk, oil and vanilla until well combined. Blend flour mixture into butter mixture, just until combined. Gently stir in 1 cup strawberries. Spoon batter evenly into the muffin cups.

Bake the cupcakes for 18 to 20 minutes or until a toothpick inserted in the center comes out clean. Let the pans cool on a rack for 10 minutes before removing cupcakes from pans to cool completely.

Meanwhile, prepare the frosting. Cream the butter until light and fluffy. Slowly add powdered sugar, beating until well mixed. Blend in vanilla and 3 tablespoons of pureed strawberries until creamy. Reserve any remaining puree for another use. Spread frosting on cupcakes. Garnish with strawberry slices.

Mandarin Coconut Delights

Makes about 12 standard cupcakes

Cupcakes

1½ C. all-purpose flour

1½ tsp. baking powder

½ tsp. baking soda

½ tsp. salt

½ C. white sugar

⅓ C. vegetable oil

1 egg

½ C. orange juice

½ C. mandarin oranges, drained

½ C. vanilla or white chocolate chips

Orange Buttercream Frosting

⅓ C. butter, softened

2 C. powdered sugar

Pinch of salt

1 tsp. grated orange zest, optional

2 T. orange juice

Coconut Topping*

Preparation

Preheat oven to 375°. Grease 12 muffin tin cups or fit the cups with paper liners.

In a large bowl, whisk together flour, baking powder, baking soda and salt; set aside. In a separate bowl, combine the sugar, oil, egg and ½ cup orange juice; mix well. Add dry ingredients to orange juice mixture and stir just until moistened. Fold in oranges and vanilla chips. Spoon batter evenly into the muffin cups.

Bake the cupcakes for 15 to 20 minutes or until a toothpick inserted in the center comes out clean. Let the pan cool on a rack for 10 minutes before removing cupcakes from pan to cool completely.

Meanwhile, prepare the frosting. Beat together butter, powdered sugar, salt, zest and 2 tablespoons orange juice until smooth. Frost cupcakes and sprinkle with Coconut Topping.

* In a skillet, melt 1 tablespoon butter. Stir in ½ cup sweetened flaked coconut and 3 tablespoons white sugar. Toast until golden brown, stirring often; let cool.

Orange Kiss-Me Cupcakes

Makes about 18 standard cupcakes

Cupcakes

2 large eggs, separated

⅛ tsp. cream of tartar

½ C. butter, softened

1 C. sugar

1 tsp. vanilla extract or orange flavoring

1¾ C. cake flour

½ tsp. salt

2½ tsp. baking powder

½ C. orange juice

Orange Frosting

3 T. butter, softened

1½ C. powdered sugar

⅛ tsp. salt

1 T. grated orange zest

2 to 3 T. orange juice

Candied Orange Zest Strips*

Preparation

Preheat oven to 350°. Grease 18 muffin tin cups or fit the cups with paper liners.

In a small mixing bowl, beat egg whites until frothy. Add cream of tartar and beat until stiff peaks form; set aside. In a medium mixing bowl, cream together butter, sugar, egg yolks and vanilla until smooth. In a separate bowl, whisk together flour, salt and baking powder. By thirds, add flour mixture and orange juice alternately to creamed mixture. Fold in beaten egg whites. Spoon batter evenly into the muffin cups.

Bake the cupcakes for 15 minutes or until a toothpick inserted in the center comes out clean. Let the pan cool on a rack for 10 minutes before removing cupcakes from pan to cool completely.

Meanwhile, prepare the frosting. Beat together all ingredients except zest strips until smooth, using enough orange juice to reach desired consistency. Spread frosting on cupcakes. Garnish with Candied Orange Zest Strips.

* Peel thin strips of orange zest from 2 oranges. Simmer strips in water for 6 minutes; drain. Combine cup water and cup sugar in saucepan and simmer strips for 15 minutes. Remove strips, cool slightly and roll in sugar. Cool completely before use.

Nutty Banana-Maple Cupcakes

Makes about 16 standard cupcakes

Cupcakes

1 (14 oz.) box banana quick bread mix

1 C. buttermilk

¼ C. vegetable oil

3 T. maple syrup

½ tsp. vanilla extract

2 large eggs

½ C. finely chopped walnuts

Maple Cream Cheese Frosting

4 oz. cream cheese, softened

2 T. butter, softened

3 T. maple syrup

½ tsp. vanilla extract

½ tsp. maple flavoring

2 C. powdered sugar

16 walnut halves

Preparation

Preheat oven to 400°. Grease 16 muffin tin cups or fit the cups with paper liners.

In a large bowl, combine bread mix, buttermilk, oil, 3 tablespoons syrup, vanilla and eggs, stirring 50 to 75 strokes or until moistened. Stir in chopped walnuts until well blended. Spoon batter evenly into the muffin cups.

Bake the cupcakes for 16 to 20 minutes or until a toothpick inserted in the center comes out clean. Let the pans cool on a rack for 5 minutes before removing cupcakes from pans to cool completely.

Meanwhile, prepare the frosting. In a small mixing bowl, beat together cream cheese, butter, 3 tablespoons syrup, vanilla and maple flavoring until smooth. Gradually add powdered sugar and beat to reach desired consistency. Spread frosting on cupcakes and place a walnut half on top. Serve promptly or refrigerate.

Sweetheart Chocolate Cupcakes

Makes about 14 standard cupcakes

Cupcakes

½ C. butter, softened

1 C. white sugar

1 egg

1 tsp. vanilla extract

1½ C. all-purpose flour

½ C. unsweetened cocoa powder

1 tsp. baking soda

¼ tsp. salt

½ C. buttermilk

½ C. strong brewed coffee or warm water

Chocolate Frosting & Candy Toppers

2¾ C. powdered sugar

6 T. unsweetened cocoa powder

6 T. butter, softened

4 to 6 T. evaporated milk

1 tsp. vanilla extract

Crushed toffee

Chocolate covered heart candies

Ready-to-use red icing in a tube

Preparation

Preheat oven to 350°. Grease 14 muffin tin cups or fit the cups with paper liners.

In a small mixing bowl, cream together butter and sugar. Beat in egg and 1 teaspoon vanilla. In a separate bowl, whisk together flour, ½ cup cocoa powder, baking soda and salt. Add flour mixture, buttermilk and coffee alternately to creamed mixture. Spoon batter evenly into the muffin cups.

Bake the cupcakes for 25 to 30 minutes or until a toothpick inserted in the center comes out clean. Let the pans cool on a rack for 10 minutes before removing cupcakes from pans to cool completely.

Meanwhile, prepare the frosting. Whisk together powdered sugar and 6 tablespoons cocoa powder; set aside. Cream butter; add powdered sugar mixture and milk alternately to butter and beat to reach desired consistency. Stir in 1 teaspoon vanilla.

Spread frosting on cupcakes. Dust with toffee and set a chocolate candy on top. Drizzle with red icing; let dry before serving.

Traditional Red Velvet Cupcakes

Makes about 24 standard cupcakes

Cupcakes

½ C. unsalted butter, softened

1½ C. white sugar

2 large eggs

3 T. unsweetened cocoa powder

2 T. red food coloring (more if desired)

2½ C. all-purpose flour

1 tsp. salt

1 C. buttermilk

1 tsp. vanilla extract

¼ C. water

1 tsp. cider vinegar

1 tsp. baking soda

Cream Cheese Frosting

1 (8 oz.) pkg. cream cheese, softened

½ C. unsalted butter, softened

1½ C. powdered sugar

1 tsp. clear vanilla extract

Tiny white nonpareils, optional

Preparation

Preheat oven to 350°. Grease 24 muffin tin cups or fit the cups with paper liners.

In a large mixing bowl, cream together ½ cup butter and sugar until fluffy. Beat in eggs. In a small bowl, make a paste of cocoa powder and food coloring; blend into creamed mixture. In a separate bowl, whisk together flour and salt; add to creamed mixture and mix well. Beat in buttermilk, vanilla and water. In a small bowl, combine vinegar and baking soda; fold vinegar mixture into cake batter just until blended. Spoon batter evenly into the muffin cups.

Bake the cupcakes for 15 to 20 minutes or until a toothpick inserted in the center comes out clean. Let the pans cool on a rack for 10 minutes before removing cupcakes from pans to cool completely.

Meanwhile, prepare the frosting. Beat together cream cheese, ½ cup butter, powdered sugar and vanilla until smooth and creamy. Spread frosting on cupcakes. Sprinkle with nonpareils, if desired. Serve promptly or refrigerate.

Out of the Blue Coconut Snowballs

Makes about 20 standard cupcakes

Cupcakes

1 (18.25 oz.) box plain white cake mix

1⅓ C. coconut milk or whole milk

2 T. vegetable oil

3 eggs

2 tsp. coconut flavoring

Whipped Cream & Coconut Topping

1 (7 oz.) bag sweetened flaked coconut

Blue food coloring

1 C. heavy or whipping cream

2 T. powdered sugar

Candy sprinkles, optional

Preparation

Preheat oven to 350°. Grease 20 muffin tin cups or fit the cups with paper liners. Place a small mixing bowl and beaters in the freezer to chill.

In a large mixing bowl, combine cake mix, milk, oil, eggs and coconut flavoring; beat until blended. Increase speed and beat for 2 minutes until well mixed. Spoon batter evenly into the muffin cups.

Bake the cupcakes for 18 to 22 minutes or until cupcakes spring back when lightly touched. Let the pans cool on a rack for 10 minutes before removing cupcakes from pans to cool completely.

Meanwhile, prepare the toppings. Place coconut in a zippered plastic bag. Add food coloring, seal bag and incorporate color by shaking and kneading bag. Spread colored coconut on a plate to dry slightly before use. Using a chilled bowl and beaters, whip the cream until slightly thickened. Gradually add sugar, beating just until soft peaks form. Do not overbeat. Spread whipped cream on cupcakes. Sprinkle generously with coconut, pressing it down gently. Top with candy sprinkles if desired. Serve promptly or refrigerate.

Cookies & Cream Cupcakes

Makes about 24 standard cupcakes

Cupcakes

1 (18.25 oz.) box plain chocolate cake mix

Eggs, oil and water as directed on box

1 (8 oz.) pkg. cream cheese, softened

1 egg

2 T. white sugar

24 bite size Oreo chocolate sandwich cookies

Toppings

2 C. whipped topping, thawed

Chocolate syrup

24 bite-size Oreo chocolate sandwich cookies

Preparation

Preheat oven to 350°. Grease 24 muffin tin cups or fit the cups with paper liners.

In large mixing bowl, combine cake mix with eggs, oil and water as directed on cake mix box; set aside. In a medium bowl, stir together cream cheese with egg and sugar until smooth and well mixed. Spoon a portion of the cake batter into the muffin cups, filling each cup no more than ½ full. Top batter with about 1½ teaspoons cream cheese mixture and 1 cookie. Use remaining cake batter to evenly cover the filling in each cupcake.

Bake cupcakes for 19 to 22 minutes or until a toothpick inserted in the center comes out clean. Let the pans cool on a rack for 10 minutes before removing cupcakes from pans to cool completely.

Just before serving, spread whipped topping over cupcakes. Drizzle with chocolate syrup and set a cookie on top.

Brownie Peanut Butter Cupcakes

Makes about 18 standard cupcakes

Cupcakes

1 (19.5) oz. box traditional fudge brownie mix

½ C. vegetable oil

¼ C. water

2 large eggs

1 C. semi-sweet chocolate chips

Peanut Butter Frosting

1 (16 oz.) can ready-to-spread vanilla frosting

¾ C. creamy peanut butter

Chocolate sprinkles or chopped chocolate chips, optional

Preparation

Preheat oven to 350°. Grease 18 muffin tin cups or fit the cups with paper liners.

In a medium bowl, combine brownie mix, oil, water and eggs, stirring until well blended. Spoon batter evenly into the muffin cups. Place a spoonful of chocolate chips in the center of batter.

Bake cupcakes for 18 to 20 minutes or until set. Let the pans cool on a rack for 10 minutes before removing cupcakes from pans to cool completely.

Meanwhile, prepare the frosting. Stir together the vanilla frosting and peanut butter until smooth. Spread frosting on cupcakes and garnish with chocolate sprinkles.

Chocolate Cherry Cupcakes

Makes about 24 standard cupcakes

Cupcakes

1 (18.25 oz.) plain devil's food cake mix

2 T. unsweetened cocoa powder

1⅓ C. buttermilk

½ C. vegetable oil

3 large eggs

1 tsp. cherry flavoring

⅓ C. finely chopped maraschino cherries, well-drained, optional

Cherry Buttercream Frosting

⅓ C. butter, softened

3 C. powdered sugar

1½ tsp. cherry flavoring

2 to 3 T. milk

Red food coloring, optional

Milk chocolate candy bars, shaved

24 whole maraschino cherries with stems, well-drained

Preparation

Preheat oven to 350°. Grease 24 muffin tin cups or fit the cups with paper liners.

In a large mixing bowl, combine the cake mix, cocoa powder, buttermilk, oil, eggs and cherry flavoring. Blend until moistened, then increase speed and beat for 2 minutes more until well mixed. Fold in chopped cherries, if desired. Spoon batter evenly into the muffin cups.

Bake the cupcakes for 16 to 20 minutes or until a toothpick inserted in the center comes out clean. Let the pans cool on a rack for 10 minutes before removing cupcakes from pans to cool completely.

Meanwhile, prepare the frosting. Cream together butter and powdered sugar. Beat in cherry flavoring, milk and food coloring to reach desired consistency and color. Spread frosting on cupcakes, sprinkle with chocolate shavings and place a cherry on top.

Cappuccino Cupcakes

Makes about 24 standard cupcakes

Cupcakes

1 (18.25 oz.) box plain yellow cake mix

Eggs, oil and water as directed on box

2 T. instant coffee powder

Cappuccino Frosting

2 T. instant coffee powder

2 tsp. hot water

1 (16 oz.) can ready-to-spread cream cheese frosting

Milk chocolate candy wafers (such as Make 'n' Mold) or kisses

Preparation

Preheat oven to 350°. Grease 24 muffin tin cups or fit the cups with paper liners.

In a large mixing bowl, combine cake mix, eggs, oil and water as directed on cake mix box, dissolving 2 tablespoons of coffee powder in the water before combining. Mix as directed. Spoon batter evenly into the muffin cups.

Bake the cupcakes for 18 to 20 minutes or until a toothpick inserted in the center comes out clean. Let the pans cool on a rack for 10 minutes before removing cupcakes from pans to cool completely.

Meanwhile, prepare the frosting. Dissolve 2 tablespoons coffee powder in hot water. Stir coffee mixture into frosting until smooth and well blended. Spread frosting on cupcakes and garnish with chocolate wafers. Serve promptly or refrigerate.

Meringue-Topped Raspberry Cupcakes

Makes about 12 standard cupcakes

Cupcakes

1½ C. all-purpose flour

1½ tsp. baking powder

¼ tsp. salt

½ C. butter, softened

¾ C. white sugar

1 large egg

2 egg yolks

3 T. raspberry juice blend

1½ tsp. vanilla extract

½ C. milk

Meringue

4 large egg whites at room temperature

¼ tsp. cream of tartar

⅔ C. white sugar

12 fresh raspberries, optional

Preparation

Preheat oven to 350°. Grease 12 muffin tin cups or fit the cups with paper liners.

In a small bowl, whisk together flour, baking powder and salt; set aside. In a large mixing bowl, cream butter; add ¾ cup sugar and beat well. Add egg, egg yolks, juice and vanilla; beat until well combined. Add flour mixture and milk alternately to creamed mixture, beating after each addition until blended. Spoon batter evenly into the muffin cups.

Bake the cupcakes for 15 minutes. Meanwhile, prepare meringue. Wash beaters thoroughly. Beat egg whites until frothy. Add cream of tartar and beat until soft peaks form. Gradually add ⅔ cup sugar, beating well until stiff peaks form.

Spread meringue on top of partially-baked cupcakes and gently press a raspberry on top of each one, if desired. Return to oven to bake for 8 to 10 minutes or until meringue is lightly browned. Let the pan cool on a rack for 5 minutes before removing cupcakes from the pan. Serve warm, or cover loosely and chill before serving.

Cookie Dough Cupcakes

Makes about 24 standard cupcakes

Cupcakes

1 (18.25 oz.) box plain yellow cake mix

1 (3.4 oz.) vanilla instant pudding mix

1 C. whole milk

1 C. vegetable oil

4 large eggs

1 tsp. vanilla extract

Refrigerated chocolate chip cookie dough, cut into 24 small pieces and frozen

Chocolate Buttercream Frosting

½ C. butter, softened

½ C. unsweetened cocoa powder

3 C. powdered sugar

1 tsp. vanilla extract

3 to 5 T. milk or half & half

Mini chocolate chip cookies

Preparation

Preheat oven to 350°. Grease 24 muffin tin cups or fit the cups with paper liners.

In a large mixing bowl, combine cake mix, pudding mix, milk, oil, eggs and vanilla. Blend until moistened, then increase speed and beat for 2 minutes more until well mixed. Spoon batter evenly into the muffin cups. Place one piece of frozen cookie dough on top of batter in each cup.

Bake the cupcakes for 23 to 27 minutes or until cupcakes spring back when lightly touched. Let the pans cool on a rack for 5 minutes before removing cupcakes from pans to cool for 15 minutes more. The centers may sink down.

Meanwhile, prepare the frosting. Cream together butter and cocoa powder. Add powdered sugar, vanilla and 3 tablespoons of milk, beating on low speed until well blended. Increase speed and beat until light and fluffy, adding more milk to reach desired consistency. Spread or pipe frosting on slightly warm cupcakes and garnish with cookies.

Cookies, Cakes, Cheesecakes & Bars

Cookies, cakes, cheesecakes and bars can be cut into a variety of shapes and sizes to create delectable desserts. Don't let the cheesecake recipes in this chapter worry you. The tips below will let you master them.

Cheesecakes Tips

✳ Purchase good quality, nonstick springform pans with easy-to-manipulate hinges on the outside.

✳ For the smoothest cheesecakes, begin with cream cheese that has been softened at room temperature. (If short on time, unwrap the cream cheese, place it in a microwave-safe bowl and warm on low power just until softened.) Beat it with an electric mixer just until smooth and creamy before adding any other ingredients.

✳ Use eggs at room temperature.

✳ If a cheesecake crust contains butter or margarine, set a jellyroll pan underneath to catch any drips during baking.

✳ Baking cheesecakes in a hot water bath may prevent cracking on top. If pans are not completely tight, securely wrap the bottom in heavy-duty foil if baking in a hot water bath. If cheesecakes are garnished, a small amount of cracking will not affect finished appearance.

✳ Most cheesecakes will settle upon cooling.

✳ To remove cheesecakes from pan, loosen outer edges with a toothpick or thin knife as needed and push up on the disk in each cup to slide the dessert out. Remove the disk before serving.

✳ Cheesecakes should be served chilled.

Cocoa Cream Thumbprints

Makes 24 cookies

Cookies

½ C. butter, softened

⅔ C. sugar

1 egg yolk

2 T. milk

1 tsp. vanilla extract

1 C. flour

⅓ C. unsweetened cocoa powder

¼ tsp. salt

Filling

2 T. butter, softened

1 (3 oz.) pkg. cream cheese, softened

½ C. powdered sugar

¼ tsp. ground cinnamon

¼ tsp. vanilla extract

Preparation

To prepare cookies, in a medium bowl, beat together butter, sugar, egg yolk, milk and vanilla until fluffy. In a small bowl, stir together flour, cocoa powder and salt; gradually add to butter mixture, beating until blended. Refrigerate dough for 1 hour or until firm enough to handle. Preheat oven to 350°. Lightly grease baking sheet. Shape dough into 1" balls. Place on prepared baking sheet. Press thumb gently into the center of each cookie or use a mini-tart shaper or the handle of a wooden spoon to make a round well in each cookie. Bake for 10 to 12 minutes or until set. Remove cookies to a wire rack; cool.

For filling, in a small bowl, beat butter and cream cheese until smooth. Add powdered sugar, cinnamon and vanilla; mix until smooth. Spoon or pipe mixture into cookies.

Big Dip Biscotti

Makes 30 pieces

Cookies

2 ¾ C. flour

1 ¾ C. sugar

1 tsp. baking powder

½ tsp. salt

3 eggs, beaten

⅓ C. creamy peanut butter

¼ to ⅓ C. water

¾ C. finely chopped peanuts

Icing & Garnish

1 ½ C. dark or milk chocolate chips

1 ½ T. creamy peanut butter

1 T. shortening

Chopped nuts, optional

Preparation

For cookies, preheat oven to 350°. Lightly coat a baking sheet with nonstick cooking spray; set aside. In a large bowl, stir together flour, sugar, baking powder and salt; set aside. In a medium bowl, beat together eggs, peanut butter and ¼ cup water until well mixed. Stir egg mixture into flour mixture until just combined. Add more water, 1 teaspoon at a time, if dough seems too dry to handle. Stir in peanuts. Divide dough into two portions and form each into a log, 3" in diameter. Place logs 3" to 4" apart on prepared baking sheet; flatten logs slightly. Bake for 40 minutes or until light brown. Remove from oven and turn off heat; cool cookies for 1 hour.

To finish cookies, preheat oven to 300°. With a serrated knife, cut logs diagonally into ½" slices. Arrange slices, cut side down, on baking sheet. Bake for 12 minutes. Flip slices over and bake for 10 to 12 minutes more. Cool completely.

For icing, in a small saucepan over low heat, melt chocolate chips, peanut butter and shortening, stirring until smooth. Dip the end of each cookie into chocolate, letting excess drip off; set on waxed paper. If desired, sprinkle with chopped nuts while wet. Let dry before serving.

Iced Treasures

Makes 14 to 18 cookies

Cookies

½ C. plus 1 T. butter, softened

½ C. sugar

1⅓ C. flour

½ C. very finely ground peanuts

Reese's miniature peanut butter cups, unwrapped and flattened*

Icing

1 oz. unsweetened or semi-sweet baking chocolate

1 T. butter

2 T. water

½ tsp. vanilla extract

1 C. powdered sugar

Preparation

For cookies, preheat oven to 350°. In a medium mixing bowl, use an electric mixer to cream together butter and sugar; beat until light and fluffy, about 2 minutes. Beat in flour and peanuts until blended. Divide dough in half. On a lightly floured surface, roll dough to ⅛" thickness (or thinner). Use a 2 ½" to 3" round cookie cutter or drinking glass to cut out circles. Set half of the dough circles on an ungreased baking sheet. Place a flattened peanut butter cup on top of each circle. Set another dough circle over peanut butter cup, with edges even; press down lightly to seal cookies together. Bake for 8 to 10 minutes or until lightly browned. Cool on baking sheets for 2 minutes before removing to a wire rack to cool completely.

To prepare icing, in a small saucepan over low heat, combine chocolate, butter and 2 tablespoons water. Cook and stir until melted. Remove from heat and stir in vanilla. Add powdered sugar and whisk together until smooth. Spread a thin layer of icing over cooled cookies; let dry.

* To flatten peanut butter cups, place between layers of waxed paper, bottom side up. Press down firmly on candy with the bottom of a spatula or the side of a knife until flat. Transfer candy to cookie tops with a spatula. If using regular–size peanut butter cups, simply slice in half horizontally and set on dough without flattening.

Sweet Cookie Pizza

Makes 10 to 12 slices

Crust

1 (14 to 18 oz.) pkg. or roll refrigerated peanut butter cookie dough

Flour

Toppings

1 C. semi-sweet chocolate chips

2 T. butter

3 T. milk

1 C. powdered sugar

Chocolate-covered peanuts, assorted chopped nuts, raisins, coconut, candy corn, mini-M&M baking bits, butterscotch baking chips and other candy toppings

2 oz. white baking chocolate, melted

Preparation

For crust, preheat oven to 350°. Set cookie dough out at room temperature for 15 minutes. Coat a 12" pizza pan with nonstick cooking spray. Press dough into prepared pan, leaving about ½" between edge of dough and pan. If necessary, sprinkle dough with a small amount of flour to minimize sticking. Bake for 11 to 15 minutes or until golden brown and set in the center. Cool in pan on a wire rack. Run a metal spatula between cookie and pan after 10 minutes to loosen.

To prepare topping, in a medium saucepan over low heat, combine chocolate chips, butter and milk just until chocolate melts, stirring occasionally. Remove from heat and stir in powdered sugar; whisk until smooth, glossy and spreadable. (If not glossy, add a few drops of hot water.) Spread chocolate over crust to within 1" of edge. Sprinkle desired toppings over chocolate, pressing lightly. Drizzle white chocolate over toppings. Let stand until set. Cut into wedges to serve.

Easy Pinwheel Cookies

Makes 60 cookies

Ingredients

1 (14 to 18 oz.) pkg. or roll refrigerated peanut butter cookie dough

¼ C. flour

1 (14 to 18 oz.) pkg. or roll refrigerated sugar cookie dough

¼ C. unsweetened cocoa powder

Preparation

In a large mixing bowl, break up peanut butter cookie dough. Add flour and stir together until combined. Divide dough in half. In another large bowl, break up sugar cookie dough; add cocoa powder and stir together to mix well. Divide dough in half. Between layers of waxed paper, roll out half of the peanut butter dough and half of the sugar cookie dough into 6" x 12" rectangles. Remove the top pieces of waxed paper. Invert one rectangle on top of the other and press down gently to seal. Remove top piece of waxed paper. Starting from one long side, tightly roll up dough into a log shape. Repeat with remaining dough portions. Wrap logs in plastic wrap and chill for 1 hour* or until firm enough to slice.

Preheat oven to 375°. Using a sharp knife, cut dough logs into slices, ¼" thick. Place slices 2" apart on an ungreased baking sheet. Bake for 8 to 10 minutes or until edges are firm. Transfer cookies to a wire rack to cool.

Dough logs may be wrapped and chilled for up to 1 week or frozen for up to 1 month. Thaw dough in the refrigerator for 3 hours before slicing and baking.

Chocolate Cream Mallows

Makes 18 sandwich cookies

Cookies

1 (1 lb., 1.5 oz.) pouch sugar cookie mix

⅓ C. unsweetened cocoa powder

2 T. flour

⅓ C. sour cream

¼ C. butter, softened

1 tsp. vanilla extract

1 egg

Filling

⅔ C. marshmallow creme

⅓ C. butter, softened

½ tsp. vanilla extract

⅔ C. powdered sugar

Preparation

Preheat oven to 350°. For cookies, in a large bowl, stir together cookie mix, cocoa powder and flour. Add sour cream, butter, vanilla and egg. With an electric mixer on medium speed, beat until a smooth, stiff dough forms. Shape dough into 36 (1¼") cookie balls. Place cookie balls 2" apart on ungreased cookie sheets. Flatten slightly using the bottom of a drinking glass dipped in sugar. Bake for 10 to 13 minutes or until set. Cool for 2 minutes; remove from baking sheets and transfer to wire racks. Cool completely.

To make filling, in a small mixing bowl, beat marshmallow creme, butter, vanilla and powdered sugar with an electric mixer on medium speed until light and fluffy. Spread about 2 teaspoons filling on flat sides of half the cookies. Top with remaining cookies, flat side down.

Sweet Pumpkin Roll

Makes 12 slices

Cake

3 eggs

1 C. sugar

¾ C. flour

¾ C. pumpkin puree

1 tsp. baking powder

1½ tsp. ground cinnamon

1 tsp. ground ginger

½ tsp. ground nutmeg

½ tsp. salt

1 tsp. lemon juice

Powdered sugar

Filling

2 (3 oz.) pkgs. cream cheese, softened

¼ C. butter, softened

1 C. powdered sugar

½ tsp. vanilla extract

½ C. finely crushed gingersnaps

Preparation

Preheat oven to 375°. For cake, line a greased 10" x 15" jellyroll pan with waxed paper; grease the paper. Set pan aside. In a medium mixing bowl, beat eggs with an electric mixer on high speed for 5 minutes. Add sugar, flour, pumpkin, baking powder, cinnamon, ginger, nutmeg and salt; mix well. Stir in lemon juice. Spread batter evenly in prepared pan. Bake for 15 minutes or until cake springs back when lightly touched. Cool for 5 minutes. Turn cake onto a kitchen towel dusted with powdered sugar. Gently peel off waxed paper. Roll up cake in towel, jellyroll style, starting with a short side. Cool completely in towel on a wire rack.

To make filling, in a large mixing bowl, beat cream cheese with an electric mixer on medium speed until smooth. Beat in butter, powdered sugar and vanilla until light and fluffy. Stir in gingersnap crumbs. To assemble, carefully unroll cake; remove towel. Spread filling over cake to within ½" of edges. Carefully re-roll and place seam side down on a serving platter. Refrigerate for at least 1 hour before serving.

Love-Filled Cake Roll

Makes 10 slices

Cake

1 (9 oz.) pkg. Jiffy yellow cake mix

¼ C. unsweetened cocoa powder

3 eggs, separated

1 T. vegetable oil

1 tsp. vanilla extract

½ C. water, divided

Powdered sugar

Filling & Garnish

¾ C. peanut butter chips

1 C. miniature marshmallows

¼ C. milk

1 C. whipping cream, chilled

½ tsp. vanilla extract

Powdered sugar, optional

Preparation

For cake, preheat oven to 375°. Line a greased 10" x 15" jellyroll pan with waxed paper; grease the paper and set aside. Stir together cake mix and cocoa powder; set aside. In a large bowl, beat egg yolks with an electric mixer on high speed for 3 minutes. Add oil, vanilla and ¼ cup water and beat on low until blended. Alternately add cocoa mixture and additional ¼ cup water to yolk mixture, beating on medium until smooth. In a separate bowl, beat egg whites until stiff peaks form; carefully fold into chocolate mixture. Spread batter in prepared pan. Bake for 12 to 15 minutes or until cake springs back when lightly touched. Invert pan on a kitchen towel dusted generously with powdered sugar. Peel off waxed paper. Roll up cake in towel, jellyroll style, starting from a short side. Place on a wire rack to cool for 1 hour.

To prepare filling, place peanut butter chips, marshmallows and milk in a microwave-safe bowl. Microwave in 30-second intervals until melted and smooth, stirring frequently; cool to room temperature. In a chilled mixing bowl with chilled beaters, use an electric mixer to beat cream until almost-stiff peaks form. Fold whipped cream and vanilla into peanut butter mixture until blended.

To assemble, carefully unroll cake and remove towel. Spread filling over cake to within ½" of edges. Re-roll cake and cover loosely; chill for at least 1 hour. To serve, sprinkle with powdered sugar or garnish as desired before slicing.

Cookies & Cream Cake

Makes 16 wedges

Cake

1 (18.25 oz.) pkg. white cake mix with pudding

1 C. water

½ C. vegetable oil

3 eggs

8 to 9 Oreos, crushed

Frosting & Garnish

3 C. whipping cream

⅓ C. powdered sugar, sifted

8 to 9 Oreos, crushed

Additional Oreos for garnish, optional

Maraschino cherries, optional

Preparation

Preheat oven to 350°. For cake, generously grease and flour two 9" round cake pans; set aside. In a large mixing bowl, blend cake mix, 1 cup water, oil and eggs with an electric mixer on low speed for 1 minute. Increase speed to medium and beat 2 minutes more. Fold in crushed Oreos. Divide batter evenly between prepared pans, smoothing out the top. Bake cakes for 28 to 32 minutes; cool on a wire rack for 10 minutes. Run a knife around the edge of each pan and invert cakes onto rack; cool completely.

For frosting, using a chilled mixing bowl and beaters, beat cream with an electric mixer on high speed until soft peaks form. Add powdered sugar and beat until stiff peaks form, about 2 to 3 minutes. Gently fold in crushed Oreos; chill. Carefully slice each cake in half horizontally. Place the bottom half of one cake layer on a serving plate, cut side up. Alternate layers of cake and whipped cream mixture, using about 1 cup whipped cream mixture between each layer. Spread remaining whipped cream mixture over the top and sides of cake, reserving a little to pipe onto cake, if desired. Garnish with reserved whipped cream, Oreos and cherries, if desired. Serve immediately.

Slow Cooker Puddin' Cake

Makes 8 to 10 servings

Cake

1 (10.25 oz.) pouch fudge brownie mix*

1 egg, lightly beaten

1 C. water, divided

¼ C. creamy peanut butter

1 T. margarine, softened

½ C. milk chocolate chips

½ C. peanut butter chips

½ C. brown sugar

2 T. unsweetened cocoa powder, optional

Topping

Vanilla ice cream or whipped topping

Preparation

Lightly coat the inside of a slow cooker with nonstick cooking spray; set aside. In a medium bowl, stir together brownie mix, egg, ¼ cup water, peanut butter and margarine until well blended. Mix in chocolate chips and peanut butter chips. Spread batter evenly in the bottom of the prepared slow cooker.

In a small saucepan over medium heat, combine ¾ cup water, brown sugar and cocoa powder, if desired (for an ultra-rich chocolate flavor). Bring mixture to a boil, stirring frequently. Pour boiling chocolate mixture over the batter in slow cooker. Cover and cook on high for 2 hours. Turn off heat and let stand for another 30 minutes. Spoon into serving dishes while warm and top with ice cream or whipped topping.

If using a 21.5-ounce box of brownie mix, use 2½ cups (about half of the mix).

Irish Cream Cheesecake

Makes 12 wedges

Crust

1¾ C. finely crushed chocolate wafers (about 30 cookies)

⅓ C. butter, melted

Filling & Garnish

4 (8 oz.) pkgs. cream cheese, softened

1 C. sugar

1 tsp. vanilla extract

4 eggs

1 T. instant coffee granules

1 T. hot water

¼ to ½ C. Irish cream

Whipped topping, thawed, optional

Chocolate-covered coffee beans, optional

Preparation

Preheat oven to 350°. For crust, in a small bowl, stir together wafer crumbs and butter. Press mixture evenly into the bottom and 2" up the sides of an ungreased 8" springform pan; chill.

To make filling, in a large mixing bowl, beat together cream cheese and sugar with an electric mixer on medium speed until smooth; add vanilla. Beat in eggs, one at a time, until well combined. In a small bowl, whisk coffee granules into 1 tablespoon hot water until dissolved; whisk in Irish cream. Gently stir coffee mixture into cream cheese mixture. Pour filling into crust. Bake for 35 to 45 minutes, until center is almost set. Cool in pan on a wire rack for 15 minutes. Run a knife or thin spatula around the edge. Let cool completely before removing pan. Refrigerate several hours before serving. To serve, remove sides of pan and slice into wedges. Top wedges with whipped topping and sprinkle with chocolate-covered coffee beans, if desired.

"Oh My!" Cheesecake Pie

Makes 12 wedges

Crust

16 Oreos, crushed

3 T. butter, melted

Filling & Garnish

3 (8 oz.) pkgs. cream cheese, softened

¾ C. sugar

1 tsp. vanilla extract

3 eggs

8 Oreos, crushed

Sweetened whipped cream, optional

Additional Oreos, optional

Preparation

Preheat oven to 350°. For crust, in a large bowl, combine crushed Oreos and butter; mix well. Press mixture firmly into the bottom of a 9" springform pan.

To prepare filling, in a large mixing bowl, beat cream cheese with an electric mixer on medium speed until smooth. Add sugar and vanilla; blend well. Beat in eggs, one at a time, beating just until blended after each addition. Gently stir in crushed Oreos. Pour batter over prepared crust. Bake for 45 minutes or until center is almost set. Cool. Run a knife or thin spatula around the edge. Refrigerate several hours before serving. To serve, remove sides of pan and slice into wedges. Serve wedges with whipped cream and additional Oreos, if desired.

Lemon Luscious Cheesecake

Makes 12 wedges

Crust

1¾ C. finely crushed lemon shortbread cookies

¼ C. brown sugar

1 tsp. grated lemon peel

½ C. butter, melted and cooled

Filling & Garnish

4 (8 oz.) pkgs. cream cheese, softened

1 C. sugar

1 C. whipping cream, divided

3 T. lemon juice

2 tsp. grated lemon peel

1 tsp. unflavored gelatin

1 T. water

Powdered sugar, optional

Preparation

Preheat oven to 350°. To make crust, in a medium bowl, combine cookie crumbs, brown sugar and lemon peel. Add butter and mix until well blended. Press crumb mixture into the bottom and 1" up the sides of a 9" springform pan. Bake for 10 minutes; cool to room temperature, about 30 minutes.

To prepare filling, in a large mixing bowl, beat cream cheese with an electric mixer on medium speed until smooth. Add sugar; beat until light and fluffy. Beat in ½ cup cream, lemon juice and lemon peel until just combined. In a small saucepan, sprinkle gelatin over 1 tablespoon water and let stand for 5 minutes. Place the saucepan over low heat and stir until gelatin dissolves; gradually whisk in remaining ½ cup cream. Add gelatin mixture to cream cheese mixture and beat until fluffy, about 1 minute. Spoon filling into cooled crust; refrigerate overnight. Sprinkle with powdered sugar, if desired. Run a knife or thin spatula around the edge of pan. Remove sides of pan and slice into wedges.

Frosty Blueberry Cream

Makes 9 squares

Ingredients

2 C. finely crushed vanilla wafers (about 60)

¼ C. butter, melted

2 C. frozen blueberries

1 C. half-and-half

¾ C. sugar

1 C. sour cream

Preparation

In a small bowl, toss together wafer crumbs and butter. Press half the mixture into an 8" x 8" pan; place blueberries over crumb mixture in pan.

In a medium bowl, whisk together half-and-half and sugar until sugar dissolves. Gradually whisk in sour cream. Pour mixture evenly over berries. Sprinkle with remaining vanilla wafer crumbs. Cover and freeze for at least 3 hours or until firm. Let stand at room temperature for 15 minutes before cutting into squares.

Frosted Shortbread Squares

Makes 48 bars

Crust

½ C. shortening

¼ C. butter, softened

⅓ C. creamy peanut butter

1 C. brown sugar

1 egg yolk

1½ tsp. vanilla extract

1¾ C. flour

Filling

1 C. creamy peanut butter

1 C. caramel topping

¼ C. sifted powdered sugar

Topping

¾ C. whipping cream

6 T. butter

3 T. light corn syrup

2 C. semi-sweet chocolate chips

¾ tsp. vanilla extract

Preparation

For crust, preheat oven to 350°. Line a 9" x 13" baking pan with foil, extending foil over edges of pan; set aside. In a large mixing bowl, use an electric mixer to cream together shortening, butter and peanut butter. Add brown sugar, egg and vanilla, beating until fluffy. Mix in flour. Press dough evenly into prepared pan. Bake for 14 to 18 minutes or until lightly browned. Cool in pan on a wire rack.

For filling layer, mix together peanut butter, caramel topping and powdered sugar until blended. Spread filling evenly over cooled crust.

To make topping, in a medium saucepan over medium heat, combine cream, butter and corn syrup; bring to a boil, stirring until dissolved and blended. Remove from heat. Add chocolate chips and vanilla to saucepan and let stand for 5 minutes without stirring; then whisk until smooth. Cool slightly. Carefully spread chocolate mixture over filling. Cover and chill for 1 to 2 hours or until chocolate layer is set. Use the foil to lift uncut bars from pan. Cut into small pieces.

Chippy Bars

Makes 36 bars

Bars

1 C. creamy peanut butter

6 T. butter, softened

1¼ C. sugar

3 eggs

1 tsp. vanilla extract

1 C. flour

¼ tsp. salt

½ C. chopped peanuts, optional

Topping

1½ C. white baking chips

1½ C. semi-sweet or milk chocolate chips

Preparation

For bars, preheat oven to 350°. In a large mixing bowl, use an electric mixer on medium speed to beat together peanut butter and butter until smooth. Beat in sugar, eggs and vanilla. Add flour and salt, beating until well mixed. Stir in peanuts, if desired. Spread batter in an ungreased 9" x 13" baking pan. Bake for 25 to 30 minutes or until edges are lightly browned.

For topping, while bars are still hot, sprinkle white chips over the top and let stand 5 to 10 minutes or until chips are shiny; spread with a knife in a thin layer over bars. Immediately sprinkle chocolate chips over the white layer, pressing lightly. Let cool completely in pan before cutting.

Dreamy Yum Yums

Makes 40 to 50 bars

Crust

1 C. flour

½ C. brown sugar

8 peanut butter sandwich cookies, crushed (1 C.)

½ C. butter, cut into pieces

¼ C. creamy peanut butter

Filling

¾ C. butter

4 C. powdered sugar

2 (3.4 oz.) pkgs. vanilla instant pudding mix

⅔ C. milk

Topping

2 C. semi-sweet chocolate chips

½ C. butter

Preparation

To make crust, preheat oven to 350°. Lightly coat a 9" x 13" baking pan with nonstick cooking spray; set aside. In a large bowl, stir together flour, brown sugar and cookie crumbs. Add butter and peanut butter; cut in with a pastry blender until mixture resembles coarse crumbs. Press mixture into the bottom and 1" up the sides of prepared pan. Bake for 13 to 15 minutes or until lightly browned. Let crust cool while preparing filling.

For filling, melt butter in a medium saucepan over low heat. Remove from heat and stir in powdered sugar, pudding mix and milk; whisk until smooth. Spread pudding mixture over crust; set aside.

To prepare topping, in a medium microwave-safe bowl, combine chocolate chips and butter. Microwave in 60-second intervals until melted and smooth, stirring often. Spread topping over pudding layer. Cover and chill for about 1 hour before cutting.

Muffins

No matter what you want in a muffin, this chapter will hook you with plenty of drool-worthy photos and crave-causing recipes to satisfy your hunger. Just follow these tips for making perfect muffins.

Muffin Tips

* Most muffin cups should be filled about ⅔ full.

* Fill jumbo muffin cups with about ⅝ cup of batter, fill standard muffin cups with about ⅓ cup batter, and fill miniature muffin cups with about 2 tablespoons batter.

* Grease muffin cups with nonstick cooking spray or use a paper towel that has been dipped in shortening to lightly grease each cup. If using paper liners, spray the insides lightly with nonstick cooking spray.

* For muffins with a rounded top, grease only the bottom and halfway up the sides of each cup.

* If some muffin cups will remain empty during baking, pour 2 to 3 tablespoons water in the unused cups to keep the pan from warping.

* If baked muffins stick to the bottom of the muffin cup, place the hot muffin pan on a wet towel for about two minutes.

* Watch muffins closely while baking. Miniature muffins will require a much shorter baking time than standard or jumbo muffins. To test doneness, stick a wooden toothpick in the top of a muffin. If no crumbs cling to the toothpick when pulled out, the muffins are done.

* Stir the wet and dry ingredients together until they are just barely mixed. Too much mixing will cause loss of leavening, resulting in muffins that don't rise.

* As soon as the batter is mixed, fill muffin cups and bake immediately.

* Both unbaked batter and baked muffins can be frozen. To freeze baked muffins, individually wrap the baked and cooled muffins in plastic wrap and place them in a freezer bag. To freeze batter, fill the muffin tins as usual and place in the freezer until the batter is frozen. Transfer the frozen batter portions to a freezer bag. To bake, place the batter portions back in a muffin tin and allow to thaw in the refrigerator before baking as normal.

Double Chocolate Chunk Muffins

*Makes 6 jumbo muffins, 12 standard muffins or
30 miniature muffins*

Ingredients

6 T. unsalted butter

4 oz. bittersweet chocolate, coarsely
chopped, divided

2 C. all-purpose flour

⅔ C. white sugar

⅓ C. unsweetened cocoa powder, sifted

1 T. baking powder

½ tsp. baking soda

½ tsp. salt

1¼ C. buttermilk

1 large egg

1 tsp. vanilla extract

Miniature chocolate chips, optional

Preparation

Place an oven rack in the center position and preheat the
oven to 375°. Grease the cups of a muffin tin or fit the cups
with paper liners.

In a double boiler over simmering water, combine the butter
and half of the bittersweet chocolate; stir until melted and
smooth. Remove the pan from the heat and set aside.

In a large bowl, whisk together the flour, sugar, cocoa powder,
baking powder, baking soda and salt; set aside. In a large
glass measuring cup, whisk together the buttermilk, egg and
vanilla. Pour the liquid ingredients over the dry ingredients;
add the melted chocolate. Stir everything together quickly
but gently. Stir in half of the remaining chopped bittersweet
chocolate. Spoon the batter evenly into the muffin cups.
Sprinkle the remaining chopped chocolate over the batter in
each cup. If desired, sprinkle some miniature chocolate chips
over the batter in each cup, as well.

Bake the muffins for 20 minutes or until a toothpick inserted
in the center comes out clean. Let the pan cool on a rack for
5 minutes before removing each muffin from its cup.

Sour Cherry Muffins

Makes 6 jumbo muffins, 12 standard muffins or 30 miniature muffins

Ingredients

2 C. all-purpose flour

1 C. plus 1 T. white sugar, divided

1 T. baking powder

1 tsp. salt

1 C. whole or 2% milk

2 large eggs, lightly beaten

½ C. unsalted butter, melted

1 T. poppy seeds

1 to 2 T. grated orange zest

1 C. dried red sour cherries

Preparation

Place an oven rack in the center position and preheat the oven to 400°. Grease the cups of a muffin tin or fit the cups with paper liners.

In a large bowl, whisk together the flour, 1 cup sugar, baking powder and salt; set aside. In a large glass measuring cup, whisk together the milk and eggs. Stir the melted butter, poppy seeds and orange zest into the milk mixture.

Form a well in the center of the dry ingredients. Pour the milk mixture into the well and fold gently until just combined. Fold in the cherries. Spoon the batter evenly into the muffin cups. Sprinkle a little of the remaining sugar over the batter in each cup.

Bake the muffins for 20 minutes or until a toothpick inserted in the center comes out clean. Let the pan cool on a rack for 5 minutes before removing each muffin from its cup.

Pumpkin Muffins with Vanilla Icing

Makes 6 jumbo muffins, 12 standard muffins or 30 miniature muffins

Muffins

1½ C. all-purpose flour

1 tsp. baking powder

1 (15 oz.) can pumpkin puree

⅓ C. vegetable oil

2 large eggs

1 tsp. pumpkin pie spice

1¼ C. plus 1 T. white sugar, divided

½ tsp. baking soda

½ tsp. salt

1 tsp. ground cinnamon

Vanilla Icing

1 C. powdered sugar

¼ tsp. clear vanilla extract

1½ T. milk

Preparation

Place an oven rack in the center position and preheat the oven to 350°. Grease the cups of a muffin tin or fit the cups with paper liners. Small ramekins can also be used.

In a large bowl, whisk together the flour and baking powder. In a separate bowl, mix together the pumpkin, oil, eggs, pumpkin pie spice, 1¼ cups sugar, baking soda and salt. Fold the dry ingredients into the pumpkin mixture; mix gently until just combined. Spoon the batter evenly into the muffin cups or ramekins.

In a small bowl, combine the cinnamon and remaining 1 tablespoon sugar; sprinkle some over the batter in each cup.

Bake the muffins for 25 minutes or until a toothpick inserted in the center comes out clean. Let the pan cool on a rack for 5 minutes before removing each muffin from its cup.

While the muffins are baking, combine the icing ingredients; stir until blended and smooth. Spoon or drizzle some of the icing over the top of each cooled muffin.

Rhubarb Buttermilk Muffins

*Makes 6 jumbo muffins, 12 standard muffins or
30 miniature muffins*

Ingredients

1½ C. finely chopped fresh rhubarb

1 T. white sugar

1 C. all-purpose flour

1 C. whole wheat flour

1 tsp. baking powder

1 tsp. baking soda

½ tsp. ground cinnamon

½ tsp. salt

1 large egg, lightly beaten

¾ C. brown sugar

2 T. canola oil

1 C. low-fat buttermilk

1 tsp. vanilla extract

Preparation

Place an oven rack in the center position and preheat the oven to 400°. Grease the cups of a muffin tin or fit the cups with paper liners.

In a large bowl, toss together the rhubarb and white sugar; set aside.

In another large bowl, whisk together both flours, baking powder, baking soda, cinnamon and salt. In a separate bowl, mix together the egg, brown sugar, oil, buttermilk and vanilla. Add the buttermilk mixture to the dry ingredients; mix until just combined. Fold in the rhubarb. Spoon the batter evenly into the muffin cups.

Bake the muffins for 15 to 20 minutes or until a toothpick inserted in the center comes out clean. Let the pan cool on a rack for 5 minutes before removing each muffin from its cup.

Blueberry Streusel Muffins

*Makes 6 jumbo muffins, 12 standard muffins or
30 miniature muffins*

Muffins

2 C. all-purpose flour

½ C. white sugar

2 tsp. baking powder

½ tsp. baking soda

½ tsp. salt

2 eggs, lightly beaten

1 (6 to 8 oz.) carton lemon yogurt

½ C. vegetable oil

1 C. fresh or frozen blueberries

Streusel Topping

⅓ C. white sugar

¼ C. all-purpose flour

2 T. butter or margarine

Preparation

Place an oven rack in the center position and preheat the oven to 400°. Grease the cups of a muffin tin or fit the cups with paper liners.

In a large bowl, whisk together the flour, sugar, baking powder, baking soda and salt. In a separate bowl, combine the eggs, yogurt and oil. Add the yogurt mixture to the dry mixture; mix until just combined. Fold in the blueberries. Spoon the batter evenly into the muffin cups.

In a small bowl, combine the streusel ingredients until crumbly. Sprinkle a portion of streusel over the batter in each cup.

Bake the muffins for 20 minutes or until a toothpick inserted in the center comes out clean. Let the pan cool on a rack for 5 minutes before removing each muffin from its cup

Muffins

Java Mocha Muffins

Makes 6 jumbo muffins, 12 standard muffins or 30 miniature muffins

Ingredients

3 large eggs

1 C. buttermilk

¾ C. canola oil

½ C. strong brewed coffee, room temperature

1 tsp. vanilla extract

1½ C. all-purpose flour

1¼ C. whole wheat flour

⅓ C. unsweetened cocoa powder

1 C. brown sugar

½ tsp. baking powder

1 tsp. baking soda

½ tsp. salt

1 C. white chocolate chips

1¼ C. chopped peanuts, divided

Preparation

Place an oven rack in the center position and preheat the oven to 375°. Grease the cups of a muffin tin or fit the cups with paper liners.

In a large bowl, whisk together the eggs, buttermilk, oil, coffee and vanilla; set aside. In a separate bowl, combine both flours, cocoa powder, brown sugar, baking powder, baking soda and salt. Mix the dry ingredients into the coffee mixture; stir until just combined. Fold in the white chocolate chips and 1 cup chopped peanuts. Spoon the batter evenly into the muffin cups.

Sprinkle some of the remaining ¼ cup chopped peanuts over the batter in each cup.

Bake the muffins for 20 to 25 minutes or until a toothpick inserted in the center comes out clean. Let the pan cool on a rack for 5 minutes before removing each muffin from its cup.

Oatmeal Raisin Cookie Muffins

Makes 6 jumbo muffins, 12 standard muffins or
30 miniature muffins

Ingredients

¼ C. butter or margarine

1 C. old-fashioned oats, divided

⅔ C. brown sugar, divided

¼ tsp. ground cinnamon

¼ tsp. ground allspice

⅔ C. water

1½ C. all-purpose flour

4 tsp. baking powder

2 tsp. wheat germ

1 large egg, lightly beaten

1 C. evaporated milk

1⅓ C. raisins

Preparation

Place an oven rack in the center position and preheat the oven to 375°. Grease the cups of a muffin tin or fit the cups with paper liners.

Melt the butter in a medium skillet over medium heat. Stir in ⅔ cup oats, ⅓ cup brown sugar, cinnamon and allspice. Heat, stirring often, until the oats are toasted and golden brown. Stir in the water and remaining ⅓ cup brown sugar; cook until slightly thickened. Remove the skillet from the heat and let cool.

In a large bowl, whisk together the flour, baking powder, wheat germ and the remaining ⅓ cup oats. In a separate bowl, whisk together the egg and evaporated milk. Form a well in the center of the dry mixture and pour the egg mixture and cooked oatmeal mixture into the center; mix until just combined. Fold in the raisins. Spoon the batter evenly into the muffin cups.

Bake the muffins for 25 minutes or until a toothpick inserted in the center comes out clean. Let the pan cool on a rack for 5 minutes before removing each muffin from its cup

Chunky Apple Breakfast Muffins

Makes 6 jumbo muffins, 12 standard muffins or 30 miniature muffins

Ingredients

2 C. all-purpose flour

¼ C. white sugar

1 T. baking powder

1 tsp. ground cinnamon

¼ tsp. salt

2 Fuji apples, peeled, cored and coarsely chopped

½ C. 1% or 2% milk

¼ C. molasses

¼ C. vegetable oil

1 large egg

1 C. raisins

Preparation

Place an oven rack in the center position and preheat the oven to 450°. Grease the cups of a muffin tin or fit the cups with paper liners.

In a large bowl, combine the flour, sugar, baking powder, cinnamon and salt. Add the chopped apples and stir until evenly mixed. In a separate bowl, whisk together the milk, molasses, oil and egg. Add the molasses mixture to the dry ingredients; mix until just combined. Fold in the raisins. Spoon the batter evenly into the muffin cups.

Bake the muffins for 5 minutes. Reduce the oven temperature to 350° and bake the muffins for an additional 15 minutes or until a toothpick inserted in the center comes out clean. Let the pan cool on a rack for 5 minutes before removing each muffin from its cup. If desired, drizzle with Vanilla Icing found on page 89.

Toffee Crunch Muffins

Makes 6 jumbo muffins, 12 standard muffins or 30 miniature muffins

Muffins

1½ C. all-purpose flour

⅓ C. brown sugar

2 tsp. baking powder

½ tsp. baking soda

½ tsp. salt

½ C. 1% or 2% milk

½ C. sour cream

3 T. butter or margarine, melted

1 large egg, lightly beaten

1 tsp. vanilla extract

3 (1.4 oz.) chocolate-covered toffee bars, finely chopped, divided

Topping

½ C. prepared white frosting

Fresh raspberries

Chocolate shavings

Preparation

Place an oven rack in the center position and preheat the oven to 400°. Grease the cups of a muffin tin or fit the cups with paper liners.

In a large bowl, combine the flour, brown sugar, baking powder, baking soda and salt. In a separate bowl, combine the milk, sour cream, butter, egg and vanilla. Add the milk mixture to the dry ingredients; mix until just combined. Fold in ⅔ of the chopped toffee bars. Spoon the batter evenly into the muffin cups.

Sprinkle the remaining chopped toffee bars over the batter in each cup.

Bake the muffins for 15 to 20 minutes or until a toothpick inserted in the center comes out clean. Let the pan cool on a rack for 5 minutes before removing each muffin from its cup.

To serve, top each cooled muffin with a dollop of the frosting. Garnish each with a raspberry and some chocolate shavings.

Raspberry Lime Muffins

Makes 6 jumbo muffins, 12 standard muffins or 30 miniature muffins

Muffins

2 C. all-purpose flour

2 tsp. baking powder

½ tsp. salt

½ C. butter or margarine, softened

¾ C. white sugar

2 large eggs, lightly beaten

1 tsp. vanilla extract

¼ tsp. grated lime zest

½ C. 1% or 2% milk

1½ C. fresh raspberries

Topping

¼ C. fresh lime juice

½ C. powdered sugar

3 T. white sugar

Preparation

Place an oven rack in the center position and preheat the oven to 375°. Grease the cups of a muffin tin or fit the cups with paper liners.

In a large bowl, combine the flour, baking powder and salt. In a separate bowl, cream together the butter and ¾ cup white sugar; stir in the eggs, vanilla and lime zest. Add the milk to the butter mixture. Add the butter mixture to the dry ingredients; mix until just combined. Gently fold in the raspberries. Spoon the batter evenly into the muffin cups.

Bake the muffins for 20 minutes or until a toothpick inserted in the center comes out clean; remove from oven and set aside. Preheat the broiler.

Meanwhile, combine the lime juice and powdered sugar; drizzle over the muffins. Sprinkle the remaining white sugar over the muffins and place under the broiler for 1 to 2 minutes, being careful not to let the muffins burn. Remove the muffins from the oven and let the pan cool on a rack for 5 minutes before removing each muffin from its cup.

Cheesy Sun-Dried Tomato Muffins

*Makes 6 jumbo muffins, 12 standard muffins or
30 miniature muffins*

Ingredients

2 C. all-purpose flour

2 tsp. baking powder

1 tsp. baking soda

Salt and pepper to taste

2 T. dried basil

2 T. crushed red pepper flakes

2 T. extra-virgin olive oil

½ C. chopped green onions

8 cloves garlic, minced

2 large eggs

1 C. cottage cheese

½ C. shredded mozzarella or Parmesan cheese

1½ C. finely chopped oil-packed,
sun-dried tomatoes

1¼ C. whole milk

¼ C. shredded cheddar cheese

2 T. poppy seeds

Preparation

Place an oven rack in the center position and preheat the oven to 350°. Grease the cups of a muffin tin or fit the cups with paper liners.

In a large bowl, sift together the flour, baking powder and baking soda. Stir in the salt, pepper, basil and red pepper flakes; set aside. Heat the oil in a large skillet over medium-high heat. Sauté the green onions and garlic until softened; set aside to cool slightly.

In a separate bowl, beat the eggs until fluffy; stir in the sautéed onions and garlic. Add the egg mixture to the dry ingredients. Fold in the cottage cheese, mozzarella cheese and sun-dried tomatoes. Slowly stir in the milk; mix until just combined. Spoon the batter evenly into the muffin cups.

Sprinkle some of the cheddar cheese and poppy seeds over the batter in each cup.

Bake the muffins for 20 minutes or until a toothpick inserted in the center comes out clean. Let the pan cool on a rack for 5 minutes before removing each muffin from its cup.

Glazed Lemon Poppy Seed Muffins

Makes 6 jumbo muffins, 12 standard muffins or 30 miniature muffins

Muffins

3 C. all-purpose flour

1 T. baking powder

½ tsp. baking soda

2 T. poppy seeds

½ tsp. salt

½ C. plus 2 T. unsalted butter, softened

1 C. white sugar

2 large eggs

1 T. grated lemon zest

1½ C. plain yogurt

Glaze

2 T. fresh lemon juice

1 C. powdered sugar

Preparation

Place an oven rack in the center position and preheat the oven to 375°. Grease the cups of a muffin tin or fit the cups with paper liners.

In a large bowl, whisk together the flour, baking powder, baking soda, poppy seeds and salt; set aside. In a separate bowl, cream together the butter and white sugar, mixing until fluffy. Add the eggs to the creamed mixture one at a time, beating well after each addition. Stir in the lemon zest. Fold in half of the dry ingredients along with one-third of the yogurt, mixing well. Add half of the remaining dry ingredients and another one-third of the yogurt. Beat in the remaining dry ingredients and yogurt; mix until just combined. Spoon the batter evenly into the muffin cups.

Bake the muffins for 20 to 25 minutes or until a toothpick inserted in the center comes out clean. Let the pan cool on a rack for 5 minutes before removing each muffin from its cup.

Meanwhile, whisk together the glaze ingredients, adding more lemon juice as needed until the glaze is a drizzling consistency. While the muffins are still slightly warm, drizzle some of the glaze over each muffin.

Pistachio Muffins

Makes 6 jumbo muffins, 12 standard muffins or
30 miniature muffins

Ingredients

1 (18.25 oz.) box yellow cake mix

1 (3 oz.) pkg. pistachio-flavored instant
pudding mix

4 large eggs, lightly beaten

1¼ C. water

¼ C. canola oil

½ tsp. almond extract

7 drops green food coloring

¼ C. finely chopped pistachios

Preparation

Place an oven rack in the center position and preheat the
oven to 350°. Grease the cups of a muffin tin or fit the cups
with paper liners.

In a large bowl, combine the cake mix, pudding mix, eggs,
water, oil and almond extract. Beat mixture with an electric
mixer at low speed until just combined. Add the green
food coloring and increase speed to medium, mixing until
thoroughly combined. Spoon the batter evenly into the
muffin cups.

Sprinkle some of the chopped pistachios over the batter in
each cup.

Bake the muffins for 20 minutes or until a toothpick inserted
in the center comes out clean. Let the pan cool on a rack for
5 minutes before removing each muffin from its cup.

Dark Chocolate Banana Nut Muffins

Makes 6 jumbo muffins, 12 standard muffins or 30 miniature muffins

Muffins

1 C. whole wheat flour

1 C. all-purpose flour

2 tsp. baking powder

1 tsp. baking soda

½ tsp. salt

½ C. plus ⅔ C. bittersweet chocolate chips, divided

½ C. chopped pecans or walnuts

¼ C. butter, softened

2 large eggs, lightly beaten

¾ C. brown sugar

½ C. unsweetened applesauce

1 banana, mashed

⅔ C. buttermilk

1 tsp. vanilla extract

Topping

2 T. unsweetened cocoa powder

1 T. plus 2 tsp. water

1 T. vegetable oil

1 T. corn syrup

1 C. powdered sugar

Banana chips

Preparation

Place an oven rack in the center position and preheat the oven to 375°. Grease the cups of a muffin tin or fit the cups with paper liners.

In a large bowl, combine both flours, baking powder, baking soda and salt; stir in ½ cup chocolate chips and nuts. In a small saucepan over very low heat, heat the remaining ⅔ cup chocolate chips and butter until melted and smooth. Remove from the heat and let cool to room temperature. In a medium bowl, whisk together the eggs, brown sugar, applesauce, banana, buttermilk, vanilla and melted chocolate mixture. Pour the chocolate mixture over the dry ingredients; mix until just combined. Spoon the batter evenly into the muffin cups.

Bake the muffins for 20 minutes or until a toothpick inserted in the center comes out clean. Let the pan cool on a rack for 5 minutes before removing each muffin from its cup.

Meanwhile, combine all topping ingredients except the powdered sugar and banana chips. Stir the powdered sugar into the mixture until a glaze forms. Top each cooled muffin with a thin layer of the chocolate glaze and garnish each with a few banana chips.

Hawaiian Island Muffins

Makes 6 jumbo muffins, 12 standard muffins or
30 miniature muffins

Muffins

1⅓ C. all-purpose flour

1 C. old-fashioned oats

1 tsp. baking powder

½ tsp. baking soda

½ tsp. salt

2 medium bananas, mashed

1 C. buttermilk

½ C. brown sugar

2 T. canola oil

1 tsp. vanilla extract

1 large egg

½ C. canned crushed pineapple in juice, drained

⅓ C. sweetened flaked coconut

3 T. finely chopped macadamia nuts, toasted

Topping

2 T. sweetened flaked coconut

1 T. finely chopped macadamia nuts

1 T. white sugar

1 T. old-fashioned oats

Preparation

Place an oven rack in the center position and preheat the oven to 400°. Grease the cups of a muffin tin or fit the cups with paper liners.

In a large bowl, combine the flour, 1 cup oats, baking powder, baking soda and salt. In a separate bowl, combine the bananas, buttermilk, brown sugar, oil, vanilla and egg. Form a well in the center of the dry ingredients. Add the banana mixture to the dry ingredients; mix until just combined. Fold in the pineapple, ⅓ cup coconut and 3 tablespoons toasted macadamia nuts. Spoon the batter evenly into the muffin cups.

In a small bowl, combine the topping ingredients. Sprinkle some of the topping over the batter in each cup.

Bake the muffins for 20 minutes or until a toothpick inserted in the center comes out clean. Let the pan cool on a rack for 5 minutes before removing each muffin from its cup.

Pies, Parfaits & Ice Cream

Have a passion for pie? Mouth watering for mousse? Fluffed-up feelings for ice cream?

Whatever your attraction, the recipes in this chapter will satisfy your desires. Give an old flame like Ice Cream Sandwiches another chance, or feel the excitement of a new love with Dreamy Creamy Tart. The pies in this chapter are easy to make because the crusts are simple, and simply delicious.

Each sweet taste will leave you longing for more!

Heart's Delight Pie

Makes 8 wedges

Crust

16 Oreos, crushed

3 to 4 T. butter, melted

Filling

1 (3 oz.) pkg. cherry-flavored gelatin powder

1 C. hot water

1 pt. vanilla ice cream, slightly softened

Whipped topping, thawed

Hershey's Kisses

Preparation

For crust, in a medium bowl, combine crushed Oreos and butter; mix well. Press mixture firmly into the bottom and up the sides of an 8" or 9" pie plate; chill.

Meanwhile, to prepare filling, in a large glass measuring cup, stir together gelatin and 1 cup hot water. Cook, uncovered in microwave, on high power for 1½ to 2 minutes; stir to dissolve gelatin. Add ice cream to the hot gelatin mixture, stirring until ice cream is completely melted. Cool slightly.

To assemble, pour ice cream mixture into pie crust. Chill for 4 hours or until set. Spoon whipped topping over entire surface of pie, smoothing as desired, and arrange Hershey's Kisses in a heart shape in the center of pie.

Cloud Nine Pie

Makes 8 wedges

Crust

1⅔ C. finely crushed animal crackers

5 T. butter, melted

1 T. honey

Filling & Garnish

1½ C. half-and-half

1½ C. coconut milk

2 eggs

¾ C. sugar

½ C. flour

¼ tsp. salt

¼ C. sweetened flaked coconut

1 tsp. coconut flavoring

Whipped topping, thawed, optional

½ C. sweetened flaked coconut, toasted,* optional

Preparation

For crust, in a small bowl, combine animal cracker crumbs, butter and honey. Press into the bottom and up the sides of a 9" pie plate.

To prepare filling, in a medium saucepan over low heat, combine half-and-half, coconut milk, eggs, sugar, flour and salt. Bring to a boil, stirring constantly. Remove from heat and stir in coconut and coconut flavoring. Pour into crust and chill for 2 to 4 hours or until firm. Spread with whipped topping and sprinkle with toasted coconut, if desired.

* To toast coconut, place in a dry pan over medium heat or on a baking sheet in a 350° oven for about 10 minutes, stirring occasionally to brown evenly.

Key Lime Pie

Makes 8 wedges

Crust

1¼ C. crushed oatmeal cookies

5 to 6 T. butter, melted

Filling

3 egg yolks

1 (14 oz.) can sweetened condensed milk

½ C. key lime juice

2 tsp. grated lime peel

Topping

1 C. whipping cream

2 T. sugar

1 tsp. grated lime peel

Preparation

For crust, in a small bowl, mix together cookies and butter. Press into the bottom and up the sides of a 9" pie or tart pan; chill.

To make filling, in a large mixing bowl, beat egg yolks with an electric mixer on medium speed until pale and fluffy, about 3 minutes. Gradually add sweetened condensed milk and beat until light and fluffy, 4 to 5 minutes. Beat in lime juice and lime peel. Pour filling into crust and bake for 10 to 15 minutes or until filling is set. Remove from oven and place on a wire rack to cool. Refrigerate until serving time.

To prepare topping at serving time, using a chilled mixing bowl and beaters, beat cream with an electric mixer on high speed until soft peaks form. Add sugar and beat until stiff peaks form. Pipe or mound whipped cream on top of pie. Sprinkle with lime peel.

Dreamy Creamy Tart

Makes 12 to 16 wedges

Crust

1 (16.5 oz.) roll refrigerated sugar cookie dough

Filling

1 (8 oz.) pkg. cream cheese, softened

1 (11.5 oz.) pkg. vanilla baking chips, melted

¼ C. whipping cream

Topping

1 to 2 bananas, sliced

1 C. fresh blackberries

1 C. fresh raspberries

3 to 4 apples or peaches, sliced

½ C. pineapple juice

¼ C. sugar

1 T. cornstarch

½ tsp. lemon juice

Preparation

For crust, preheat oven to 300°. Pat cookie dough into the bottom of a greased 12" pizza pan. Bake for 25 to 28 minutes or until lightly browned; cool.

To make filling, in a medium mixing bowl, beat cream cheese with an electric mixer on medium speed until smooth. Add melted baking chips and cream; beat until smooth. Spread filling mixture over crust. Chill for 30 minutes.

For topping, arrange bananas, blackberries, raspberries and apples over filling. In a small saucepan over medium heat, combine pineapple juice, sugar, cornstarch and lemon juice; bring to a boil over medium heat. Boil for 2 minutes or until thickened, stirring constantly. Cool; brush over fruit. Chill for 1 hour before serving.

Creamy Mousse Pie

Makes 8 to 10 wedges

Crust
....

1 (14 oz.) can sweetened condensed milk, divided

⅔ C. semi-sweet chocolate chips

1 (9") graham cracker crust

Filling
....

1 (8 oz.) pkg. cream cheese, softened

1 C. creamy peanut butter

2 C. whipped topping, thawed

Additional whipped topping, optional

Preparation
....

For crust, in a medium microwave-safe bowl, combine ⅓ cup sweetened condensed milk and chocolate chips. Microwave for 30 seconds and stir until smooth. Repeat if necessary. Place 2 tablespoons of mixture in a resealable plastic bag and set aside for drizzling. Spread remaining chocolate mixture over bottom of prepared crust. Chill for 10 minutes.

To make filling, in a large mixing bowl, combine remaining milk, cream cheese and peanut butter. Using an electric mixer on medium speed, beat until smooth. Stir in 2 cups whipped topping until blended. Spread filling over chocolate layer in crust and freeze for 1 hour. Before serving, spread or dollop additional whipped topping over pie, if desired. Cut pie into wedges. Warm up the bag of reserved chocolate in a bowl of warm water for several minutes to achieve a drizzling consistency. Snip off one corner of bag and drizzle chocolate over pie wedges.

White Chocolate Decadence

Makes 6 parfaits

Parfaits

6 oz. white baking chocolate

1½ C. whipping cream, divided

½ C. sugar

1 tsp. orange juice

4 C. fresh raspberries

24 shortbread cookies

Garnish

Powdered sugar, optional

Preparation

In a small microwave-safe bowl, microwave white chocolate and ¼ cup cream until chocolate is melted; stir until blended. Cool to room temperature.

Using a chilled mixing bowl and beaters, beat remaining 1¼ cups cream with an electric mixer on high speed until soft peaks form. Fold into cooled chocolate mixture. In a medium bowl, combine sugar and orange juice. Add raspberries and toss gently to combine.

Break cookies into bite-size pieces. In each of six parfait or wine glasses, alternate layers of broken cookies, white chocolate mixture and raspberries; repeat. Garnish by sifting powdered sugar over each serving, if desired. Serve immediately.

Double Rich Mousse

Makes 6 to 10 servings

Mousse

3 oz. unsweetened baking chocolate

¾ C. water

¾ C. plus 3 T. sugar, divided

⅛ tsp. salt

3 egg yolks

2¼ tsp. vanilla extract, divided

1¾ C. whipping cream

6 Oreos, finely crushed

Garnish

Sweetened whipped cream, optional

Additional Oreos, coarsely chopped, optional

Preparation

In a medium saucepan over low heat, combine chocolate with ¾ cup water, stirring until melted and smooth. Stir in ¾ cup sugar and salt. Bring to a boil over medium heat, stirring constantly. Reduce heat and simmer for 5 minutes, stirring constantly.

In a small bowl, whisk egg yolks. Blend a small amount of hot mixture into egg yolks. Stir egg yolk mixture back into hot mixture in saucepan. Cook and stir for 1 minute. Remove from heat and cool to room temperature. Stir in 1½ teaspoons vanilla and crushed Oreos.

In a medium mixing bowl, beat whipping cream, 3 tablespoons sugar and ¾ teaspoon vanilla with an electric mixer on high speed until soft peaks form. Fold into cooled chocolate mixture. Spoon mixture into individual dishes. Add a dollop of whipped cream and chopped Oreos, if desired.

Banana Pudding Parfaits

Makes 6 parfaits

Ingredients

⅔ C. sugar

¼ C. cornstarch

¼ tsp. salt

2½ C. milk

4 egg yolks

2 T. butter, cut into pieces

1 tsp. vanilla extract

2 bananas

¼ C. lemon juice

12 vanilla cream-filled cookies, coarsely crushed

½ C. whipping cream

1 T. sugar

Preparation

In a medium saucepan on a cold stove, whisk together sugar, cornstarch and salt. Gradually whisk in milk, a few tablespoons at a time, until cornstarch is dissolved; whisk in egg yolks. Cook mixture over medium heat, whisking constantly, until mixture just begins to boil. Reduce heat to low. Cook for 1 minute, whisking constantly. Remove from heat and pour through a sieve into a medium bowl. Stir butter and vanilla into hot pudding.

Let mixture cool slightly. Divide pudding mixture equally into six parfait glasses; refrigerate for about 1 hour or until set. Slice bananas. In a small bowl, mix lemon juice and bananas; drain. Layer bananas and cookies over pudding mixture. In a small mixing bowl with an electric mixer on high speed, beat whipping cream and sugar until soft peaks form. Spoon whipped cream over the top of the parfaits.

Chippy Cream Sandwiches

Makes 17 to 20 sandwiches

Cookies

2 ¼ C. flour

1 tsp. baking soda

¾ C. brown sugar

½ C. butter, softened

½ C. shortening

¼ C. sugar

1 (3.4 oz.) pkg. vanilla instant pudding mix

1 tsp. vanilla extract

⅛ tsp. almond extract

2 eggs

2 C. semi-sweet chocolate chips

Filling

½ gal. chocolate ice cream, slightly softened

Preparation

Preheat oven to 350°. To make cookies, in a small bowl, stir together flour and baking soda. In a large mixing bowl, cream together brown sugar, butter, shortening, sugar, pudding mix, vanilla and almond extract with an electric mixer on medium speed until well blended. Add eggs, one at a time, mixing well after each addition. Gradually add flour mixture to batter, mixing until well blended. Stir in chocolate chips. Drop by rounded teaspoonfuls on an ungreased baking sheet. Bake for 10 to 12 minutes. Cookies will be soft. Remove to a wire rack to cool.

For filling, soften ice cream slightly. Place desired amount of ice cream on the flat side of half the cookies. Cover with remaining cookies, flat side down. Push down lightly. Using a knife, smooth the edges of ice cream. Place on a baking sheet in the freezer until ice cream is solid. Remove from freezer and wrap individually in aluminum foil. Return to freezer until ready to serve.

Luscious Layered Bombe

Makes 12 wedges

Bombe

1 (1.75 qt.) carton chocolate ice cream

3 C. peanut butter cookie ice cream*

6 fun-size Snickers candy bars

8 peanut butter sandwich
cookies, crushed (1 C.)

Topping

1 (7.25 oz.) bottle Reese's chocolate & peanut
butter shell ice cream topping

Preparation

Coat an 8- to 10-cup bowl with nonstick cooking spray; line bowl with plastic wrap, extending plastic over sides by about 8". Open carton of chocolate ice cream; cut ¾"-thick slices of ice cream. Place slices in bowl to cover bottom and side to 1" from top, cutting as needed to fit snugly. With the back of a large spoon, press down to fill gaps and make smooth. Freeze for 20 minutes or until firm. Meanwhile, soften peanut butter cookie ice cream slightly. Cut candy bars into ¼"-thick slices. Stir candy into ice cream. Spoon ice cream into bowl on top of chocolate layer and spread level. Sprinkle cookie crumbs over the top, pressing lightly into ice cream. Fold plastic wrap over bowl and freeze overnight or up to 2 weeks.

Up to one day before serving, remove bowl from freezer and uncover. Set a wire rack over a rimmed baking sheet. Place a cardboard round over crumbs and invert bombe and cardboard together onto a wire rack. Remove bowl and plastic wrap. Quickly smooth out any wrinkles on ice cream with the back of a warmed spoon; refreeze for 10 minutes. Pour most of shell coating over bombe, letting it drizzle over the sides as desired and spreading quickly with a large offset spatula to cover. Garnish with a drizzle of remaining coating. Transfer to a serving platter and freeze until serving time. Cut into wedges with a warm knife.

* If not available, soften 3 cups vanilla ice cream and mix in ⅓ cup creamy peanut butter.

Ice Cream Sandwiches

Makes 6 sandwiches

Cookies

½ C. margarine*, softened

1 C. brown sugar

2 eggs

1 tsp. vanilla extract

½ C. unsweetened cocoa powder

2 C. flour

1 tsp. baking powder

¼ tsp. salt

Filling

½ gal. vanilla ice cream, slightly softened

Preparation

To prepare cookies, in a medium mixing bowl, cream together margarine and brown sugar with an electric mixer on medium speed. Beat in eggs, one at a time, until well combined; stir in vanilla. In a small bowl, combine cocoa powder, flour, baking powder and salt. Gradually stir dry ingredients into margarine mixture to combine. Form dough into a ball; chill for 1 hour. Preheat oven to 375°. On a floured surface, roll dough to ¼" thickness. Using a sharp knife, cut out pieces about 2¼" x 5". Transfer to an ungreased baking sheet. Using the tines of a fork or a round toothpick, poke designs in the rectangles. Bake for 8 to 10 minutes or until set. Place on a wire rack to cool completely.

For filling, cut rectangular blocks from ice cream about the size of the cookies and ½" thick; freeze until solid. To assemble, place one cooled cookie, top side down, on a flat work surface followed by one ice cream block and another cookie, top side up. Trim ice cream with a knife, if desired. Wrap sandwich in foil; place in freezer. Repeat with remaining cookies and ice cream blocks. Freeze several hours before serving.

* Using margarine produces a soft, chewy cookie.

Lovely Freezer Pleaser

Makes 12 to 16 wedges

Crust

30 Oreo cookies

6 T. butter, melted

¾ C. fudge topping, at room temperature

Filling & Garnishes

1 pt. chocolate ice cream, softened

3 pts. vanilla ice cream with choice of stir-ins*

½ C. creamy peanut butter, warmed

Caramel topping

Whipped topping

Chocolate candy bars, cut up

Preparation

To make crust, lightly coat a 9" or 10" springform pan with nonstick cooking spray. Use a rolling pin to crush cookies into fine crumbs. In a medium bowl, combine crumbs and butter. Press crumb mixture into the bottom and partway up the side of prepared pan; freeze for 10 minutes. Remove from freezer and spread fudge topping over the crust. Freeze for 15 minutes.

For filling, spread chocolate ice cream over crust and fudge layer; freeze for at least 30 minutes. Place softened vanilla ice cream (with stir-ins) in a large bowl; add peanut butter and stir until well blended. Spread peanut butter ice cream over chocolate ice cream layer. Cover and return to freezer for 4 hours or overnight. Remove springform pan; spread dessert with caramel topping. Cut into wedges with a warm knife and garnish as desired with whipped topping and pieces of chocolate candy.

* Stir approximately 1½ cups of one or more of these chopped items into softened vanilla ice cream: chocolate chips, peanut butter chips, chocolate baking chunks, chocolate-covered peanuts or Reese's peanut butter cups. You may also use purchased flavored ice cream such as chocolate chunk, peanut butter cup or chocolate chip cookie dough ice cream.

Cool Cookie Pops

Makes 10 pops

Ingredients

1 (3.9 oz.) pkg. chocolate instant pudding mix

2 C. milk

6 Oreos, crushed

½ C. whipped topping, thawed

Preparation

In a medium bowl, whisk together pudding mix and milk, about 2 minutes. Add crushed Oreos and whipped topping; stir to blend. Spoon mixture into ten 3-ounce paper or plastic cups. Insert a wooden popsicle stick or plastic spoon into each. Freeze about 5 hours or until firm. Remove from freezer. Hold each cup in your hands for a few seconds. Carefully hold wooden stick while pulling to remove cup.

Berry Creamwiches

Makes 15 to 18 sandwiches

Cookies

⅔ C. shortening

⅔ C. margarine, softened

1½ C. sugar

2 eggs, slightly beaten

3½ C. flour

1 tsp. salt

2 tsp. baking powder

2 tsp. vanilla extract

Filling

½ gal. berry or cherry ice cream, slightly softened

Preparation

Preheat oven to 375°. For cookies, in a large mixing bowl, mix together shortening, margarine, sugar and eggs with an electric mixer on low speed until creamy. In a small bowl, stir together flour, salt, baking powder and vanilla. Add to shortening mixture. Mix on medium speed until well blended. On a floured surface, roll dough to about ¼" thick. Using a 2¾" square cookie cutter, cut as many cookies as possible. Place on an ungreased 10" x 15" baking sheet. Re-roll and cut remaining dough; add to baking sheet. Bake for 8 to 10 minutes or until just set and lightly browned. Do not overbake. Remove from pan and cool completely on wire rack.

For filling, remove ice cream from carton and cut into squares slightly smaller than the cookies and about ½" to ¾" thick. Carefully place one square of ice cream on flat sides of half the cookies. Cover with remaining cookies, flat side down. Push down lightly. Wrap individually in aluminum foil; freeze several hours before serving.

Peanut Butter Cup Milkshake

Makes 2 large servings

Milkshake

2 C. milk

2 C. vanilla ice cream*

6 T. creamy peanut butter

¼ C. chocolate syrup

2 peanut butter cups, cut up

Garnishes

Sweetened whipped cream (recipe below)

Additional peanut butter cups, fudge sauce, graham cracker crumbs, optional

Preparation

In a blender container, combine milk, ice cream, peanut butter, chocolate syrup and peanut butter cups. Blend until very smooth. Immediately pour into serving glasses and top with whipped cream.

Garnish with peanut butter cups, fudge sauce and a sprinkling of graham cracker crumbs, if desired.

* For more chocolate flavor, use chocolate ice cream instead of vanilla.

Sweetened Whipped Cream

1 C. heavy or whipping cream

½ tsp. vanilla or almond extract

2 T. sugar

Approximately 30 minutes before preparing, chill a medium mixing bowl and the beaters of an electric mixer. To prepare, pour cream and vanilla into chilled bowl. Beat until mixed. Add sugar and beat on medium speed until soft peaks form. Mound on top of milkshakes (or other desserts) just before serving. Makes 2 cups.

Garnishing with Flair!

Garnishes can turn plain desserts into impressive party-perfect presentations! Just follow these simple instructions and suggestions.

To Make Chocolate Filigrees

Line a baking sheet with waxed paper. In a microwave-safe bowl, melt ¾ cup chocolate candy wafers or almond bark until smooth. Spoon melted chocolate into a plastic bag or waxed paper cone (or use a piping bag with a small round tip). Cut off one corner for piping. Pipe small shapes, such as hearts, free-form designs or letters, on a waxed paper-lined baking sheet. Chill in the freezer for 30 minutes or let stand undisturbed at room temperature until set. Carefully peel the designs off the waxed paper and set them lightly in whipped topping or frosting to garnish the tops of desserts.

To Pipe on Toppings, Mousse or Frostings

Fit a plastic piping bag (pastry or decorating) with a large star tip. Fill bag with sweetened whipped cream, whipped topping, mousse or thick frosting. Squeeze bag to pipe desired topping on desserts in patterns, swirls or mounds. To do this with a plastic food storage bag, fill the bag and cut off a medium to large piece from one corner and then squeeze bag to pipe topping.

To Drizzle Chocolate

Melt ⅓ cup white or dark chocolate chips with ½ teaspoon vegetable oil in a microwave-safe bowl, stirring until smooth. Spoon mixture into a plastic bag and cut a tiny piece off one corner of the bag to drizzle fine lines of chocolate back and forth over the top of desserts.

To Add Frosted Texture to Brownies

Coat brownies generously with the frosting and then drag the tines of a fork through it in a back-and-forth or wavy motion to add lines.

To Create Layers

Slice cheesecakes or brownie cubes into two layers and spread filling or frosting between them. Freeze before coating in chocolate. Garnish as desired.

Index

brownies. *See* cake pops & bites

cake pops & bites, 8–50
about: brownie tips, 8
Black & White Cut-Ups, 44
Blueberry Cheesecake Fudge Minis, 47
Bon Bon Delights, 19
Brownie Bomb Pops, 32–33
Checkerboard Brownie Bomb Pops (variation: Mint Brownie), 33
Chocolate & Mint Cheesecake Bites, 18
Chocolate-Covered Cheesecake Pops, 10–11
Chocolate-Covered Cherry Cheesecake Bits, 34
Cookie Crust Cheesecakes (cheesecake variations: Chocolate Chip; Oreo; Peanut Butter; Chocolate; Spice), 38–39
Cool Cookie Pops, 115
Cranberry Blondies, 17
Dainty Mocha Cheesecake Baskets, 26
Double-Dipped Blondie Pops, 24–25
Fudge Jewels, 29
German Chocolate Brownie Pops (variations: Milk Chocolate; Quick Caramel), 48–49
Lime Cheesecake Mini Tarts (variations: Mini Wedges; Bites), 40–41
Little Rocky Roads, 50
Milk Chocolate Malt Cheesecakes, 14
No-Bake Mandarin Orange Tartlets, 27
No-Bake Pumpkin Wedges, 35
Orange-Kissed Brownie Wedges, 16
Peanut Butter Cheesecake Pops, 20–21
Peppermint Brownie Pops, 12–13
Rainbow Blondie Party Pops, 37
Raspberry Swirl Cheesecake Cubes, 22–23
Strawberry Cheesecake Minis, 36
Surprise Brownie Babies, 15
Tantalizing Truffles, 28
Tiki Bar Volcanoes (variations: Grasshopper; Strawberry/Raspberry Daiquiri), 42–43
Tingly Mint Fudge, 9
Tiny Turtle Cheesecakes, 46
Triangle Treats, 45
Triple Chocolate Cheesecake Wedges (variations: Peppermint; Raspberry), 30–31

cakes & rolls, 75–78. *See also* cheesecakes
Cookies & Cream Cake, 77
Love-Filled Cake Roll, 76
Slow Cooker Puddin' Cake, 78
Sweet Pumpkin Roll, 75

cheesecakes, 79–81
about: tips for making, 68
Irish Cream Cheesecake, 79
Lemon Luscious Cheesecake, 81
"Oh My!" Cheesecake Pie, 80

cookies & bars. *See also* cake pops & bites
Big Dip Biscotti, 70
Chippy Bars, 84
Chocolate Cream Mallows, 74
Cocoa Cream Thumbprints, 69
Dreamy Yum Yums, 85
Easy Pinwheel Cookies, 73
Frosted Shortbread Squares, 83
Frosty Blueberry Cream, 82
Iced Treasures, 71
Sweet Cookie Pizza, 72

cupcakes, 51–67
about: tips for making, 51
Brownie Peanut Butter Cupcakes, 63
Cappuccino Cupcakes, 65
Carnival Poke Cupcakes, 53
Chocolate Cherry Cupcakes, 64
Cookie Dough Cupcakes, 67
Cookies & Cream Cupcakes, 62
Luscious Lemonade Cupcakes, 54
Mandarin Coconut Delights, 56
Meringue-Topped Raspberry Cupcakes, 66
Milky Way Sweetcakes, 52
Nutty Banana-Maple Cupcakes, 58
Orange Kiss-Me Cupcakes, 57
Out of the Blue Coconut Snowballs, 61
Scrumptious Strawberry Cupcakes, 55
Sweetheart Chocolate Cupcakes, 59
Traditional Red Velvet Cupcakes, 60

garnishes, 118

muffins, 86–101
about: tips for making, 86
Blueberry Streusel Muffins, 91
Cheesy Sun-Dried Tomato Muffins, 97
Chunky Apple Breakfast Muffins, 94
Dark Chocolate Banana Nut Muffins, 100
Double Chocolate Chunk Muffins, 87
Glazed Lemon Poppy Seed Muffins, 98
Hawaiian Island Muffins, 101
Java Mocha Muffins, 92
Oatmeal Raisin Cookie Muffins, 93
Pistachio Muffins, 99
Pumpkin Muffins with Vanilla Icing, 89
Raspberry Lime Muffins, 96
Rhubarb Buttermilk Muffins, 90
Sour Cherry Muffins, 88
Toffee Crunch Muffins, 95

pies, parfaits & ice cream. *See also* cheesecakes
about: overview of, 102
Banana Pudding Parfaits, 110
Berry Creamwiches, 116
Chippy Cream Sandwiches, 111
Cloud Nine Pie, 104
Cool Cookie Pops, 115
Creamy Mousse Pie, 107
Double Rich Mousse, 109
Dreamy Creamy Tart, 106
Heart's Delight Pie, 103
Ice Cream Sandwiches, 113
Key Lime Pie, 105
Lovely Freezer Pleaser, 114
Luscious Layered Bombe, 112
Peanut Butter Cup Milkshake, 117
White Chocolate Decadence, 108

whipped cream, sweetened, 117

More Great Books from Fox Chapel Publishing

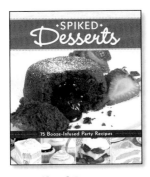

Spiked Desserts
ISBN: 978-1-56523-722-3 **$14.95**

Cooking for the Man Cave
978-1-56523-740-7 **$14.99**

Grilling Gone Wild
978-1-56523-725-4 **$14.95**

Treasured Amish and Mennonite Recipes
ISBN: 978-1-56523-599-1 **$19.95**

Edible Party Bouquets
ISBN:978-1-56523-723-0 **$14.95**

Making Sparkling Wines at Home
ISBN: 978-1-56523-690-5 **$12.95**

Easy Campfire Cooking
ISBN:978-1-56523-724-7 **$12.95**

Simply Paper Cutting
978-1-57421-418-5 **$19.99**

Real Cidermaking on a Small Scale
978-1-56523-604-2 **$12.95**